The War of 1812

Western New York Public Broadcasting Association
Horizons Plaza
P.O. Box 1263
Buffalo, New York 14240
(716) 845-7000
www.wned.org

Library of Congress Control Number: 2011934407

ISBN: 978-1-59652-8307

Printed in the United States
11 12 13 14 15 16 17—1 2 3 4 5 6 7

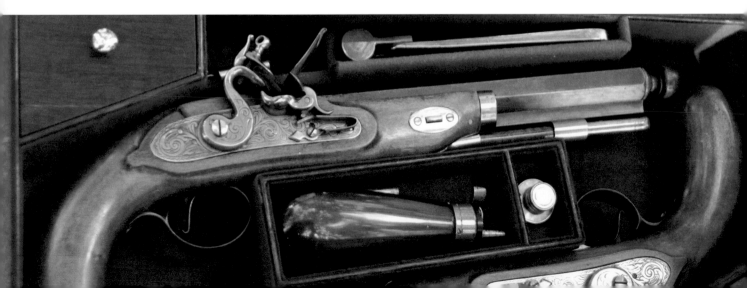

COMPANION TO THE ⬤ PBS₀ TELEVISION SPECIAL

A GUIDE TO BATTLEFIELDS AND HISTORIC SITES

The War of 1812

JOHN GRANT AND RAY JONES

Table of Contents

Foreword

FROM THE COASTS OF MAINE and New Brunswick in the east, through the Great Lakes, and westward as far as the Pacific extends what is surely the friendliest international boundary in the world: the border between the United States and Canada. One may easily imagine that it has always been as peaceable as it is today. But the fact is that 200 years ago, the people on either side of that border took up arms against one another in a legendary struggle known as the War of 1812.

The War of 1812 was an event of immense importance, one destined to shape the political geography of North America. It was also an intensely violent affair. Stout forts were blasted with cannon and rockets; towns and villages were devastated; storehouses and government buildings were burned; and thousands of brave men and women were killed or maimed. Then, little more than two and a half years after it began, the fighting ended.

Many generations have come and gone since a thin line of Canadian militiamen made their brave stand at Chateauguay, the USS *Constitution* defeated the frigate HMS *Guerrière* in the North Atlantic, the British captured Washington and burned the White House, Native Nations leader Tecumseh lost his life in battle, and Andrew Jackson's outnumbered army of misfits successfully defended New Orleans. Despite the passage of two centuries, however, the War of 1812 is once more a timely topic of discussion for schoolchildren and adults on both sides of the Atlantic and both sides of the U.S. and Canadian border. Indeed, the bicentennial of the war has sparked a full-blown revival of interest in this smoky, old cannon and musket conflict.

Adding to the excitement is a colorful new PBS documentary, *The War of 1812*, a coproduction of WNED, Buffalo/Toronto and Florentine Films/Hott Productions in association with WETA, Washington, D.C. The documentary allows viewers to relive this epic event and to understand how and why it happened and what it all meant.

For the benefit of viewers and others who want to learn even more about this extraordinary chapter in North American and British history, John Grant, Ray Jones, and WNED have compiled this fascinating companion book. *The War of 1812: A Guide to Battlefields and Historic Sites* encourages travelers to visit the actual woodlands, meadows, riverbanks, and fortresses where the war was fought. Visitors will find that this book and the venerable battlefields, monuments, and other historic sites it describes will enable them to see the war at a basic human level—as if through the eyes of the men and women who fought and died in it. Like the documentary, the book tells the story of the war from several points of view: American, Canadian, Native American, and British.

In a sense, this multiple perspective is a reflection of WNED's bi-national commitment. We serve viewers throughout Western New York and Southern Ontario, embracing our shared history, exploring what makes us unique, and renewing our present and future bond as national neighbors.

We thank all our viewers for helping support fine public television programs and projects such as *The War of 1812* documentary and *The War of 1812: A Guide to Battlefields and Historic Sites*. Our special thanks also to our generous program funders, all of whom are listed elsewhere in this book. Without their generosity, programs like *The War of 1812* would not be possible. Finally, we extend our appreciation to PBS for its continued support and enthusiasm for this project.

Thanks also go to executive producer John Grant, producers Larry Hott, Diane Garey, writer Ken Chowder, and narrator Joe Mantegna for the outstanding job on the television production; WNED's David Rotterman and WETA's Karen Kenton; and to Ray Jones and John Grant for supplementing the program with detailed information on the U.S. and Canadian historic and battlefield sites included in this book.

Our hope is that those on both sides of the border will enjoy this companion book and the documentary as a way of celebrating our shared national history and heritage.

Donald K. Boswell
President and CEO, WNED-TV

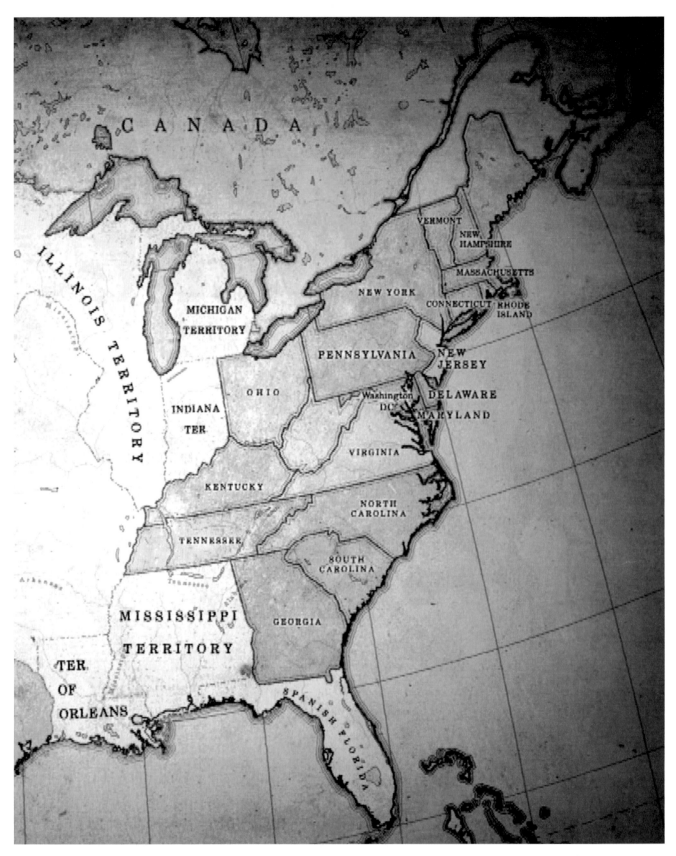

During the early nineteenth century, North America consisted largely of wilderness with much of the population concentrated in the east and along the St. Lawrence River. During the War of 1812, American, British, Canadian, and Native tribal forces fought for control of the vast lands and resources in the west. Indeed, the war would shape the political and cultural destiny of the entire continent.

Introduction

THE WAR THAT SHAPED A CONTINENT

ON JUNE 17, 1812, THE UNITED STATES SENATE took one of the most momentous votes in American legislative history. With all thirty-two senators present and voting, it approved by a surprisingly slim margin of 19 to 13 a measure that had been passed by a similarly divided House of Representatives two weeks earlier. Then, having been approved by a seemingly halfhearted Congress, the bill was sent along to President James Madison for his signature.

It has been said that Madison's face was "white as a sheet" when, on the following day, he dipped a quill pen in ink and prepared to put his name on the document. The president's pallor was all too understandable since the bill before him was nothing less than a declaration of war against Great Britain, which was then the most powerful nation on earth. In population, in financial and industrial resources, in international standing, and, most

A sharply divided U.S. Congress votes to declare war on Great Britain. President James Madison then signs the declaration, and the War of 1812 begins with the stroke of a pen.

importantly, in military might, the fledgling United States was a pygmy compared to its new enemy. Madison knew this, but even so, he signed the declaration. Thus began the War of 1812—not with the roar of cannon on the high seas, the crack of muskets in the field, or the tramping feet of an invading army—but with the stroke of a pen.

Although the War of 1812 began in relative calm with an act of legislation, it was destined to break like a storm over the North American continent and the oceans of the world. The bitterly fought and widespread conflict was marked by 13 invasions and dozens of blood-drenched battles. Fighting flared along the international border from Detroit on the north-western frontier to Plattsburgh in upstate New York, on the shores of the Chesapeake outside Baltimore and Washington, D.C., in Native American villages of the Midwest and South, and at the gates of New Orleans in Louisiana. There were also fierce maritime battles on Lakes Erie, Ontario, and Champlain and on the high seas off Virginia, Massachusetts, Nova Scotia, Cuba, Ireland, the Azores, the Canaries, British Guyana, Brazil, and even in the South Pacific near Chile.

Indeed, the scope of the war would prove far greater and its consequences more far-reaching than anything President Madison might have imagined when he and the Congress plunged their country into it. They had counted on a limited conflict, which they fervently hoped would last only a few months and end in victory. Instead, the war would go on for more than two-and-a-half brutal and bloody years and conclude indecisively. Before the fighting came to an end, America's tiny army and navy and its inexperienced militia would be tested to the breaking point, the U.S. Capitol would be put to the torch, and Madison himself would be burned out of house and home. In the course of these trials, the bonds that held the nation together would be stretched to the limit and its very existence called into question.

The years of war would challenge America's opponents as well. The peoples of Upper and Lower Canada and Britain's other North American provinces would find them-selves thrust onto the war's frontlines struggling desperately to stave off invasion and absorption by a far more populous United States. Having failed in their effort to estab-lish a unified Indian nation, the Native American tribes of the Midwest and South would be devastated and would lose their last, best chance to preserve a way of life that was uniquely their own. Even the British, who at first regarded the war as little more than an annoyance, found it a deeply trying experience. Not only was the all-powerful Royal Navy repeatedly embarrassed at sea by America's fast frigates, but the fighting in North America siphoned off resources urgently needed for the war against Napoleon in Europe. It also threatened to unravel the British Empire by ripping away Britain's remaining North American colonies.

The War of 1812 produced death and destruction, like all wars do, but not on a cataclysmic scale. Total American, British, Canadian, and Native American battle casualties likely did not exceed 25,000. These losses were quite small compared to those of the Napoleonic wars then being fought in Europe. For instance, in a single battle fought on September 7, 1812 at Borodino outside Moscow, more than 70,000 French and Russian soldiers were killed or wounded. Some 60,000 British, French, and Prussian troops fell during the 1815 Battle of Waterloo, which brought to a close the Napoleonic era.

The Leopard's *attack on the American frigate* Chesapeake *in 1807 helped set the stage for war. A few years later the* Chesapeake *would lose another key sea battle, this time with the British frigate* Shannon, *shown here unleashing a punishing broadside.*

When the War of 1812 ended after the signing of the Treaty of Ghent on Christmas Eve in 1814 and the Battle of New Orleans—fought several weeks after treaty terms had been agreed upon—it seemed as if little had changed. Under the terms of the treaty, the borders of the United States, Upper Canada, and Lower Canada, remained just as they had been before the war. Relations between the United States and Great Britain returned to what they had been during most of the decades since the Revolution—commercially vigorous but politically wary. And yet, the long-term consequences of what some at the time referred to sneeringly as "Mr. Madison's War" turned out to be enormous.

The war reaffirmed Britain's willingness and ability to defend its Empire, a far-flung economic and political titan that would continue to dominate the world for nearly another century and a half. At the same time, the war made the United States a respected player, albeit a minor one, on the world stage. Despite all the military setbacks and hardships it

Depicted here standing tall at the Battle of Lundy's Lane, British regulars and Canadian militia blunted several American invasion thrusts, ensuring that Canada would remain permanently separate from the United States.

had heaped upon them, the war gave Americans a more confident sense of themselves and of their national destiny. By clearing away the last real chance that a unified Indian nation might emerge in the West, it opened the way for U.S. expansion all the way to the Pacific. The war also helped define Canada as a nation distinct from the United States and, in time, from Great Britain as well. Canada would never again be seriously threatened by its more populous neighbor to the south and eventually would evolve into a vast nation of ten provinces and three territories stretching from the Atlantic to the Pacific. In short, the War of 1812 shaped North American political geography as we know it today.

United States and Canada in 1812

In 1812, the United States consisted of 17 states and a number of territories. Among the latter was the Louisiana Territory, which had been purchased from Napoleon's France in 1803 and had extended U.S. holdings all the way to the Pacific. The U.S. population at that time was about 7.7 million (including more than a million slaves) and it was growing at an extraordinary rate, perhaps as much as 30 percent each decade. Since most Americans were farmers, the pressure to open up new lands for settlement was increasing year by year. This, in turn, ignited conflict with Native American tribes along the frontier.

During the early nineteenth century, Britain's North American colonies included Upper Canada (Ontario), Lower Canada (Quebec), Nova Scotia, and New Brunswick. Although the Canadas in particular were vast in land area, the total population of all four provinces was only about 500,000, roughly 7 percent of that of the United States. Many Canadians were French-speaking farmers whose ancestors had settled in the St. Lawrence Valley before France ceded Canada to the British following the French and Indian War. Many others were British loyalists who had moved north after the United States won its independence in the Revolutionary War. The relatively small and diverse population of these British possessions made them a tempting target in the eyes of expansion-minded Americans such as Henry Clay who mistakenly believed that many, if not most Canadians, would side with the United States in any confrontation with Great Britain.

HOW AND WHY DID IT HAPPEN?

In all of human history 1812 stands out as the only year that has a war named after it. This may be because the causes of the war have never been clearly understood. No single sweeping expression like "the defense of liberty" or "the abolition of slavery" was ever put forward to define its purpose. The war had a variety of causes both real and imagined, and hostilities had simmered for years along the American frontier, at sea, and in the minds of American and British politicians and ordinary citizens.

During the decade leading up to the war, Britain was engaged in a colossal struggle with Napoleon's France. In much the way the twentieth-century British would later think of Adolf Hitler, the early nineteenth-century British saw Napoleon as a monster on the verge of devouring the world. Regarding themselves as the defenders of civilization, they were prepared to do whatever was necessary to defeat the French Emperor. Among the most important tactics the British employed in their war against Napoleon was an economic blockade of continental Europe. Established under a parliamentary act called Orders in Council, the blockade was

As the nineteenth century dawned, white settlers were already pushing into the Midwest where they encroached on lands held by various Native American tribes.

designed to prevent neutral ships and goods from reaching ports controlled by the French. The blockade placed severe hardships on neutral shippers and generated considerable resentment among U.S. maritime interests, although not enough to bring about open conflict.

However, policing the blockade required the British to maintain the largest navy on the planet—more than 1,000 ships—and not surprisingly, they often ran short of able-bodied seamen. Undermanned British warships often stopped neutral vessels and took the sailors they needed by force. Sometimes the British captains claimed these impressed seamen were not foreign citizens at all but rather Royal Navy seamen who had jumped ship to seek an easier, less regimented life on neutral vessels. This was a distinction lost on Americans who regarded the impressment of their seamen, whether or not they were actually U.S. citizens, as an utter outrage—a just and sufficient cause for war.

Some say that the first shots of the war were fired not in 1812 but five years earlier off the coast of Virginia. On the afternoon of June 22, 1807, HMS *Leopard*, a heavily armed British frigate overtook the U.S. frigate *Chesapeake*, ordering it to "heave to" and allow a British search party to board her. The commander of the *Chesapeake*, Commodore James Barron, refused. Unfortunately for Commodore Barron and his crew, they were neither expecting nor prepared for a battle. The *Chesapeake's* gun ports were lashed shut and her decks cluttered with supplies just brought on board in preparation for a long cruise.

Moments after receiving the *Chesapeake's* negative reply, Captain Salisbury Humphreys on the *Leopard* ordered his gunners to open fire. For ten long minutes the *Leopard* raked the helpless American vessel with broadside after broadside. The fierce cannonade killed three *Chesapeake* seamen and injured eighteen others, including Barron, who soon struck his colors in defeat.

A British boarding party then came aboard the *Chesapeake* and removed four sailors, who had in fact previously served on Royal Navy warships. One, a British citizen, was hung from the yardarms. The other three, all U.S. citizens, were later returned in an attempt by the British to defuse the furor the incident had generated. The British government also agreed to pay reparations for the damage done to the *Chesapeake*, but this did little to sooth the severely strained relations with their former colonies.

Thomas Jefferson, then in his second term as President, sought to defuse the situation and redress American grievances through negotiations. When talks ultimately proved fruitless, Jefferson turned to a form of economic warfare. As a response to the Orders in Council and to similar restrictive measures imposed by the French, the United States placed an embargo on all international trade moving in or out of American ports. It was thought this would force the belligerents across the Atlantic to recognize the vital importance of trade with the United States and to respect freedom of the seas and the right of free trade. Instead, the worst effects of the embargo were felt not overseas but in America where merchants and farmers, unable to export their goods and produce, were impoverished.

Having failed to produce the desired results, the embargo was lifted in 1809, but the U.S. economy did not quickly recover. Ironically, the economic hard times the embargo and similar measures had caused would prove among the chief contributing factors to the war fever that had overtaken America by 1812. Southerners and Westerners in particular hoped that a war might somehow open up the world to their products and revitalize the American economy. Of course, there were also other important factors at work.

A Shawnee chief, Tecumseh hoped to assemble a powerful Indian confederacy capable of resisting the flood of white settlers.

Governor William Henry Harrison used whatever means were necessary to acquire Indian lands for white settlement.

TROUBLE ON THE FRONTIER

On August 12, 1810 two remarkable individuals met face to face at Vincennes, the capital of the Indiana Territory. One was Tecumseh, a Shawnee chief and a man of immense energy and vision. The other was William Henry Harrison, a strong-willed pioneer politician. The two men were soon to become blood enemies.

As the appointed governor of the territory, Harrison was attempting to open the region to settlement by purchasing large tracts of land from various Native American tribes. It has been said that at times Harrison's bargaining tactics included bribes, bullying, whisky, deceit, and outright fraud. For certain he was none too particular about whether those who sold him land had actually owned it in the first place.

In the summer of 1810, Tecumseh and Harrison met for talks at Vincennes on the Midwestern frontier. It was obvious the two men, along with the cultural and military forces they led, were on a collision course.

Tecumseh, whose name meant "Shooting Star" in Shawnee, challenged Harrison's right to acquire Indian lands in this manner. To counter Harrison and help his people hold back the tide of white settlers from the East, Tecumseh began to organize a confederacy of tribes with himself at its head. Seeing trouble on the horizon, Harrison invited Tecumseh to his mansion in Vincennes for talks. The invitation called for Tecumseh to bring no more than thirty followers. The Shawnee brought more than twice that number.

Tecumseh had frank words for Harrison. "I now wish you to listen to me," said the chief. "I tell you so because I alone am authorized by all the tribes to do so. I am the head of them all. We want to establish a principle that the lands should be considered common property and none sold without the consent of all."

Tecumseh deeply impressed Harrison who would later describe him this way: "He is one of those uncommon geniuses which spring up occasionally to produce revolutions and over-turn the established order of things. If it were not for the vicinity of the United States, he would perhaps be the founder of an empire. No difficulties deter him. Wherever he goes he makes an impression favorable to his purpose."

Having learned that Tecumseh was away from his home base at Prophetstown, Harrison marched on the village with a sizeable force. This led to the Battle of Tippecanoe, which Harrison later trumpeted as a great victory.

However, the parlay produced no positive results, and Tecumseh would soon be inciting tribes all along the frontier to take up arms against the whites. "The Great Spirit said he gave this great island to his red children," Tecumseh told his people. "He placed the whites on the other side of the big water, but they were not content with their own, and they came to take ours from us. They have driven us from the sea to the lakes; we can go no farther."

Recognizing that Tecumseh might soon grow too strong to stop, Harrison resolved to move against him. Picking a time when the great chief himself was away drumming up support, Harrison assembled a force of about 1,100 U.S. regulars and militia and marched into Indian country. His objective was Prophetstown, Tecumseh's home village and the focus of the confederacy movement.

On the night of November 6, 1811, Harrison and his troops pitched camp on the banks of Tippecanoe Creek about 2 miles from Prophetstown. Early the next morning, as the soldiers slept they were attacked by a large Indian war party led by Tecumseh's brother, a shaman and seer widely known as the Prophet. Although mauled by the Prophet's warriors, Harrison's men eventually beat back the assault with gunfire and bayonets, and on the following day, they entered Prophetstown.

Before burning the village and large quantities of food and supplies, they made a startling discovery: muskets that appeared to have been obtained from the British. Although it has never been clear whether the weapons had been given to the Indians by the British or had been purchased from traders, Harrison was convinced that the British were arming tribes throughout the West and encouraging them to attack white settlements.

News of the battle spread like wildfire across the frontier and then to the East where city journals accepted Harrison's claims as gospel. Soon newspapers were crying out for retaliation against the British. One headline shouted: "The blood of our fellow citizens murdered by British intrigue calls aloud for vengeance!" In Washington the clamor emboldened a group of eager young Congressmen who were prepared to stake their careers and their very lives if necessary on an extraordinary gamble—war against mighty Great Britain.

WAR HAWKS

From the beginning, political power in the United States had been split between the more urban northern states, which had already begun to industrialize, and the more rural and agrarian South. At first, the Federalist Party championed by John Adams, Alexander Hamilton, and other northern political leaders held the upper hand. By the turn of the nineteenth-century, however, the steady growth of population in the West, where small farmers felt they had little in common with the Federalists, tipped the balance in favor of the South.

With the election of Virginia's Thomas Jefferson in 1800, the more Southern- and Western-oriented Democratic Republican Party was swept into power. Jefferson and his allies in Congress cut taxes and reduced the nation's military to a few scattered regiments and a dozen or so armed naval vessels. At the same time, Jefferson pursued an expansionist policy, and in 1803 he concluded the Louisiana Purchase, which theoretically at least, practically doubled the size of the country. To integrate these vast new domains into the nation as a whole would take generations of settlement, a process that could not begin so long as hostile Native American tribes stood in the way. Opening the door on the West would require a larger and more capable military and a greater willingness to fight than Jefferson demonstrated during his eight years as President.

President James Madison

War Hawk Henry Clay

War Hawk John C. Calhoun

In 1809 Jefferson's close friend James Madison became President. A studious and retiring man, Madison at first appeared even less anxious than Jefferson had been to go to war.

However, the elections of 1810 brought to Congress a number of passionate young firebrands, such as Henry Clay of Kentucky and John C. Calhoun of South Carolina, who would come to be known as the War Hawks. Politicians of a whole new breed, they had all reached manhood long after the Revolution and were far less likely than their predecessors to consider the grim consequences of war. Instead, they saw in it a grand adventure.

"I would take the whole continent from Britain," said Clay, who was a brilliant orator as well as a devotee of social soirees, fat cigars, and all-night poker games. "I wish never to see peace until we do."

Although they were nearly all members of Madison's own party, the War Hawks worked hard to outmaneuver him in Congress. In time, it would seem they even managed to win the President over to their point of view. They apparently convinced him that war was the nation's only honorable response to British insults at sea and meddling in the West. On June 1, 1812, Madison surprised the nation by delivering to Congress a strongly worded message

Militia in the United States and Canada

During the War of 1812, both sides relied heavily on militia—farmers, shopkeepers, and other citizen soldiers who in times of danger traded in their plows and aprons for muskets. Recruited and controlled by individual states, the U.S. militia forces often proved ineffective on the battlefield. This was due in part to poor or nonexistent prewar training and in part to the antiwar sentiment of some state militias. In fact, some American militiamen adamantly refused to cross the border and invade British territory. On the other hand, Canadian militiamen, who saw themselves as defending their homes and families against an unprovoked attack, were more often successful. In the October 1813 Battle of Chateauguay, for instance, a thin line of 1,400 French- and English-speaking Canadian militiamen drove back an American army more than twice its size.

calling for war with Great Britain. Acting in accordance with the war powers granted them under the U.S. Constitution, the War Hawks and their allies in Congress then replied with an official declaration of war.

A MERE MATTER OF MARCHING

Beginning in earnest just a few weeks after Madison signed the declaration and proclaimed that a state of war existed between the United States and Britain, the War of 1812 would be a multi-sided struggle. It involved several more or less separate factions, each with its own reasons for taking part in the conflict. These reasons were not always clear even to those doing the fighting.

In the United States, the War Hawks and other supporters of the war said they intended to defend the honor and the sovereign rights of their nation, especially on the high seas. But of course, they wanted much more than that. Not only were they resolved to defeat the Indians in the West and open the frontier to more rapid settlement, but they had also set their sights on Canada. With its rich resources and nearly endless expanse unsettled land, Canada seemed a plum ripe for the picking, especially with the British distracted by their war against Napoleon.

Napoleon Bonaparte won numerous victories in Europe. Many Americans assumed incorrectly that the British were too hard-pressed by the French Emperor's rampaging armies to mount a successful defense of Canada.

Thomas Jefferson, for one, was quite optimistic: "The acquisition of Canada this year, as far as Quebec, will be a mere matter of marching, and will give us experience for the attack on Nova Scotia the next, and the final expulsion of England from the American continent. Canada wants to enter the Union."

However, if Jefferson and others in America thought the Canadians were likely to welcome them with open arms, they would soon be bitterly disappointed. Most Canadians, even French-speaking ones who had less reason than most for remaining loyal to the British crown, eyed their neighbors to the south with deep suspicion. While some may have been uncertain of their own national identity and of their proper place within the British Empire, Canadians were nearly unanimous in their determination to remain separate from the United States. As a consequence, whenever U.S. forces crossed the border, they were regarded as invaders and in nearly every case beaten back by a Canadian militia more than willing to serve under British officers.

To the British government and military, the war with the United States was initially less a direct threat than a nuisance. For the first two years of the war the British were of necessity almost entirely focused on their drive to defeat the much hated and feared Napoleon.

After Napoleon's fall from power in April 1814, however, the British were able to turn their full attention to North America. They would pursue several key goals in doing so. First and foremost they intended to force the Americans to accept a negotiated settlement while punishing them for the temerity of declaring war on Great Britain. This, in turn, would remove the U.S. threat to Canada. In these primary objectives the British would prove at least partially successful.

The British also hoped to obstruct the western expansion of their troublesome former colonies and bottle them up to the east of the Alleghenies. To accomplish this they sought to encourage the emergence in the Midwest of an armed and organized Indian nation, one capable of resisting the westward march of white settlement. In these secondary objectives the British were destined to fail.

Doomed along with British ambitions to extend their influence over the American western frontier were their Indian allies. In fighting alongside the British, Tecumseh and other Native Americans hoped to defend their tribal lands and preserve their traditional ways. Likely they understood only too well that they were, in fact, fighting for their very survival. Sadly for the Indians, it was a battle they never really had a chance to win.

THEATERS OF CONFLICT

The War of 1812 drama was played out in several distinct theaters, and the fighting in each was not often directly related to what was going on in other areas. There was a War of 1812 in the Northwest near the shores of Lakes Erie, Michigan, and Huron. There was a war along the Niagara River, and a war on Lake Ontario, Lake Champlain, and in the St. Lawrence River Valley. There was a war in New England and Nova Scotia and a war in and along the Chesapeake Bay. There was a war in the Deep South, and there was a war at sea.

Within each of these theaters, the fighting surged back and forth with one side enjoying success for a while and then the other. Many of the skirmishes and pitched battles in one or another theater would have no real impact on the outcome of the war as a whole. Yet, each and every armed confrontation, whether minor or of great strategic significance, was always a matter of life or death to the troops and civilians caught up in the fighting. And it would leave an indelible impression on them. Even years after the war had ended some would look back upon the war with a mixture of horror, fear, and anger.

Superior training and tactics placed highly disciplined British regulars at a significant advantage when they confronted inexperienced American troops in the field.

"I thought hell had broken loose and let her dogs of war upon us," said one American remembering a counterattack by British, Canadian, and Native American forces at the Battle of Queenston Heights.

"The Cannon began to roar apparently with tenfold fury," said Lydia Bacon, caught in the bombardment of Fort Detroit. "A 24-pound shot cut two officers who were standing in the entry directly in two, their bowels gushing out."

"Whenever the Americans got any of our people into their hands," said a Potawatomi war chief, "they cut them like meat into small pieces."

"Of all the sights that I ever witnessed, that which met me there was beyond comparison the most shocking and the most humiliating," said George Gleig, a British officer haunted by the slaughter of his countrymen at the Battle of New Orleans. "Within the narrow compass of a few hundred yards were gathered together nearly a thousand bodies, arrayed in British uniforms.... An American officer stood by smoking a cigar with a look of savage exultation."

Many of the fiercest battles took place not in the West, South, or at sea but within a few dozen miles of the existing U.S.-Canadian border. In fact, the war would prove to be mostly about Canada—U.S. attempts to conquer Britain's Canadian provinces and the mostly successful British efforts to throw the Americans back across the border. Early U.S. invasions of Canada were easily repulsed. Although nearly always outnumbered, mixed forces consisting of small contingents of British regulars, Canadian militia, and Indians frequently pummeled the overconfident Americans. On the other hand, British sorties across the border onto U.S. soil invariably failed to produce decisive results.

Both sides enjoyed greater successes and suffered more profound defeats when the fighting shifted away from border areas. It might be argued that the outcome of the war was decided not on the Canadian border but along the shores of the Chesapeake Bay. By capturing Washington and burning the U.S. capital in November 1814, the British impressed upon one and all that the Americans would not and could not win the war. And yet, when the British attempted to drive home their advantage a few weeks later by capturing the vital commercial center of Baltimore, they were repulsed. This mixed result in the Chesapeake convinced both sides that the war would most likely end in a stalemate.

The fighting at sea also failed to produce a clear decision. Early in the war, America's speedy frigates stunned the Royal Navy by winning several hard-fought ship-to-ship engagements. American warships and privateers also placed pressure on Britain by raiding commercial shipping. However, the overwhelmingly outnumbered U.S. Navy could not hope to break the British blockade of the U.S. ports which, in time, became so tight that it all but strangled the American economy.

Only in the South did the United States win clear-cut military victories with long-lasting consequences. There General Andrew Jackson vanquished a renegade faction of Creek Indians and then went on to badly mangle a British invasion force outside New Orleans in one of America's few convincing triumphs of the war. Ironically, Jackson's defeat of the British at the Battle of New Orleans took place several weeks after negotiators in Europe had already agreed to make peace.

Although the British won most of their battles in North America, they were soundly defeated by Andrew Jackson's ragtag army at Chalmette Plantation outside New Orleans. Ironically, the Battle of New Orleans was fought several weeks after peace negotiators had settled on terms at Ghent, Belgium.

TROUBLE ON THE HOME FRONT

In 1813 and 1814, as the war entered its second and then its third years, the peoples of the warring nations grew increasingly weary of the conflict. In the United States the war threatened to tear apart the constitutional union of states. Mostly Federalist in their sympathies, New Englanders had never been enthusiastic about fighting the British. Although New England shippers and seamen had resented the British Orders in Council and highhandedness at sea, the wartime blockade of northeastern ports had cost them far greater suffering. They wanted out, if not from the war, then from the Union itself.

In the fall of 1814, as the war took a decided turn against the Americans, New Englanders began to speak openly of secession. Only a week after the burning of Washington, the Massachusetts legislature called for a special convention to "amend the constitution." Many Americans, including President Madison, believed that the real purpose of the convention was to break the New England states away from the Union, form a new nation, and make a separate peace with the British. As it turned out, convention delegates did not meet until December 1814, and by then the fortunes of war had shifted again—this time in America's favor—and that in turn had rallied support for the war. As a result, when the delegates from Massachusetts, Connecticut, Rhode Island, New Hampshire, and Vermont finally came together at Hartford, they passed a lot of tough-sounding resolutions but uttered not a word on the subject of succession.

Meanwhile, the British had internal troubles of their own. Great Britain had been at war for more than 20 years, first against Revolutionary France, then against Napoleon, and finally, against the United States. British citizens were being crushed by a mountain of wartime debts and taxes. They wanted the war brought to a swift conclusion, if not by military means, then through a negotiated settlement.

Having driven Napoleon out of power, the British were able to focus their military might on the United States. To force the Americans to capitulate and accept peace on British terms, they launched three separate invasions of the United States, one each from the north, east, and south. The invasion forces consisted of hardened veterans who had fought Napoleon in Europe. With the support of the all-powerful Royal Navy, they might have cut America to pieces, but as things turned out, they didn't. Moving down from Canada along the shores of Lake Champlain the first invasion was turned back at Plattsburgh. Concentrating on the Chesapeake, a second British force managed to capture and burn Washington but could not break through into the more important commercial city of Baltimore. The third invasion attempt was destined to meet with disaster outside New Orleans.

PEACE HAWKS

In August 1814, peace negotiations between the United States and Britain had gotten underway in the city of Ghent, Belgium. At first, the British did not appear interested in a settlement, and they sent low-ranking commissioners to Ghent. After all, they seemed to have the upper hand on the battlefield. Following their reversals at Plattsburgh and Baltimore, however, they began to take the talks more seriously.

The peace treaty concluded at Ghent, Belgium, on Christmas Eve in 1814 was intended to restore the status quo, but the War of 1812 would have enormous long-term consequences, especially for the United States and Canada.

"If we had either burnt Baltimore or held Plattsburgh, I believe we should have had peace on our terms," said British commissioner Henry Goulburn. "But as things appear to be going on in America, the result of our negotiations may be very different."

The United States had selected as its peace commissioners the most capable men it had available. Among the American commissioners were the eloquent John Quincy Adams, who would later become the sixth U.S. President, and Albert Gallatin, who had served as Secretary of the Treasury for more than a dozen years. Also on hand was Henry Clay, whose fiery speeches had helped start the war. Now Clay and the others threw themselves with equal passion into an effort to stop it.

Although these were supposed to be peace *talks,* weeks would pass with very little talk of any kind. Through the late summer and autumn of 1814, negotiators for the two sides rarely met. They had gotten stuck on the question of the territorial concessions demanded by Great Britain. For themselves, the British wanted Maine plus free access to the Mississippi River. For their Indian allies, they wanted nearly all the western Great Lakes region, an area encompassing what would later become the states of Indiana, Illinois, Wisconsin, and Michigan. Even Ohio, which had already entered the Union as the seventeenth state, appeared on the list of British territorial demands. These concessions were, of course, totally unacceptable to the Americans.

As the fall wore on, the British began to soften their hard-line stance. Ohio would remain part of the United States. So would Maine, and the issue of access to the Mississippi was tabled. Then a major breakthrough opened the door to a final and lasting agreement. Instead of setting aside a clearly defined territory for the Indians, the treaty returned to them the lands they had held prior to the war. This was a provision that could and would later be interpreted exactly as the American government wished.

With the thorny issue of Indian lands out of the way, negotiations moved steadily forward. On December 24, Christmas Eve, they were concluded and the Treaty of Ghent was signed by members of the two delegations. The treaty was swiftly approved by governments on both sides of the Atlantic, though not before several regiments of British regulars began their fateful march toward the gaping muzzles of Andrew Jackson's lethal cannon at New Orleans.

Essentially, the treaty restored the state of affairs that existed before the war. Borders remained fixed and no territory changed hands. Ironically, the treaty did not even mention trading rights and the impressment of seamen. The fall of Napoleon had rendered those issues irrelevant. Indeed, it seemed as if nothing at all of substance had changed, but that could not have been further from the truth.

OH SAY CAN YOU SEE?

Two centuries have now passed since the events described in this book took place. Although, time provides perspective, it rarely clarifies our view of wars and similar national upheavals. Generally speaking, wars are remembered indistinctly through veils of myth or outright ignorance, and this is especially true of the War of 1812.

Georgetown lawyer Francis Scott Key enshrined the war's most enduring image with his poem "The Star-Spangled Banner." It describes the British bombardment of Fort McHenry near Baltimore and the giant American battle flag he could see still flying there at dawn.

Americans nearly always study the war at some point in their school careers, but by the time they reach adulthood, they forget much of what they have learned. For instance, they may be only vaguely aware that their national anthem is, in fact, a celebration of the War of 1812. They may know by heart the words of "The Star-Spangled Banner" and still not recall that the "rocket's red glare" once brightened the skies over Fort McHenry. Baseball fans in Kansas City, Denver, or Seattle sing the song with enthusiasm before each game without the slightest inkling that these major league cities might never have existed if the War of 1812 had not been fought. The United States of America owes much of its length, breadth, prosperity, and confident spirit to a war that modern Americans have all but forgotten.

"Who were we fighting, anyway?" they may ask. "Were we involved in that war, or was it only the British and Napoleon? What was it all about anyway?"

Canadians are far less likely to ask such questions. They know exactly who and why their ancestors were fighting. They were fighting Americans, who had invaded their country for no apparent reason, and to remain separate from a seemingly alien and hostile United States. The Canadians succeeded in repelling not one but several American invasions, with the result that Canada would remain for generations to come a part of the British Empire. Never again would the United States make a claim on Canadian territory or sovereignty. Perhaps for those reasons the War of 1812 remains to this day a deeply ingrained part of Canada's national identity.

For the British, on the other hand, the War of 1812 is little more than a historical footnote. For them it was a sideshow, an unwanted distraction from the far more important global war against Napoleon. Like their American cousins, British children are taught about the war in school but much of what they learn is soon forgotten.

Native American children who study the War of 1812 may do so with a deep sense of confusion, and perhaps, of loss. Although, their ancestors fought side by side with the British and Canadians on blood-soaked battlefields throughout the Midwest, the war did not enable them to establish a strong, independent nation of their own.

For the Indians, the war was a calamity, and the treaty that ended the conflict left them with little means to resist the westward expansion of white farmers and white culture. So, America's indigenous peoples may see little cause to celebrate the war—or to sing about it.

Many, if not most, Americans are unaware that the "Star-Spangled Banner" is not only their nation's national anthem but also a celebration of the War of 1812.

While others may have claimed victory in the war, America's Native peoples clearly lost. This very stylized print depicts the fall of Native American hero Tecumseh during the October 5, 1813 Battle of the Thames in Canada.

WE TOOK A LITTLE TRIP

In 1959 a country and western song became so popular that its lyrics were on the lips of nearly every American. Young people especially could be heard singing the words with a march-like staccato rhythm: "In 1814 we took a little trip...." The song was called *The Battle of New Orleans.*

The song had been written by Jimmy Driftwood, an Arkansas high school teacher, to help his students learn about their nation's complex history. He had found that, while they might know quite a bit about the Revolutionary War, the Civil War, World War II, or the more recent Korean War, they knew almost nothing about the War of 1812. They weren't very interested in it either. So Driftwood—who worked as a professional musician on the side— wrote *The Battle of New Orleans* and played it for them in the classroom. Somehow country and western star Johnny Horton heard about the song and added it to his act. His version of *The Battle of New Orleans* won a 1959 Grammy Award.

The Battle of New Orleans was not just wildly popular in America but also in Britain. However, British music lovers found the song more than a little perplexing. What was all this about a war between Great Britain and the United States? And was it possible that an army of professional British regulars had been vanquished by a scruffy band of American frontiersmen? Some of them turned to their history books and discovered that, well, yes it was possible.

During the late 1950s, Jimmy Driftwood's song sparked a reawakening of interest in the War of 1812. It was a short-lived curiosity, however, one that would soon be submerged by the cultural tumult of the 1960s and by another divisive conflict—the Vietnam War. Nevertheless, many British, Canadians, and Americans remember *The Battle of New Orleans* and more than a few can still hum the tune.

ABOUT THIS BOOK

The men and women for whom the War of 1812 was most important—those who fought it—passed away long ago. Their great-grandchildren have passed away as well. Those great-grandchildren may have living grandchildren, but they would be very old by now.

A long time has passed since British regulars and Canadian militiamen made their successful stand at Crysler's Farm, the USS *Constitution* defeated the frigate HMS *Java* off the coast of Brazil, the British captured and burned Washington, and the garrison at Fort McHenry weathered a blizzard of Royal Navy shot and shell. Even so, the War of 1812 is once more on the minds of the American, Canadian, Native, and British peoples. The bicentennial of the war has sparked a revival of interest. So, too, has the PBS documentary *The War of 1812,* a coproduction of WNED, Buffalo/Toronto and Florentine Films/Hott Productions in association with WETA, Washington. The documentary allows viewers to relive this epic international struggle and invites them to consider the enormous impact it had on the world as we know it today. It is our sincere hope that this book will likewise help to awaken new interest in this extraordinary chapter in North American and British history.

To truly understand a world-changing historical event such as the War of 1812, and to dispel the myths associated with it, one must learn about it at a basic human level. An excellent

Shown here in an antique photograph taken many years after the conflict subsided, these grand old warriors fought for the British during the War of 1812. Their war cries may have been heard at Queenston Heights, Lundy's Lane, and elsewhere along the Niagara frontier.

way to bring the war down to human size and at the same time grasp its immense historical importance is to visit the battlefields and other relevant sites that date from the era of the conflict. How better to learn about the war than to see it as ordinary soldiers and citizens did from the woods and meadows of the Chippawa Battlefield, the summit of Queenston Heights, the ramparts of Fort McHenry, or the gun galleries of the USS *Constitution*? *1812: A Guide to Battlefields and Historic Sites* is meant to encourage travelers to visit these and many other fascinating places closely linked to the War of 1812.

After this Introduction, the book is divided into seven chapters, each including an expanded listing of major battlefields and historic sites. Each of the main chapters focuses on one of several distinct theaters of the war: Northwest, Niagara, Lake Ontario, St. Lawrence/ Champlain, Northeast, Chesapeake, and Southern. These theaters and the chapters related to them progress geographically in a clockwise fashion from west to east and then to the south. As it happens, the war itself developed somewhat in the same fashion. The opening battles were fought in and around Detroit in what was then the far-off Northwest. Later on the focus of the conflict shifted eastward to the banks of the Niagara and the shores of Lake Ontario. In the last year of the war many of the key battles were fought along the Chesapeake Bay or in the South.

Within each chapter, battlefields and historic sites are listed in approximate chronological order according to the dates of important events. This enables readers to follow the course of the war and of battlefield action just as it unfolded in each theater. Individual listings explain what happened and why that was important to the war as a whole. Each listing explains what you will discover if you visit these revered historic locations today. It also offers advice on how to enjoy your visit and take from it a deeper appreciation of the War of 1812, one of the most interesting—yet poorly understood—conflicts in human history.

Like other wars, the War of 1812 is often recalled through a haze of dreamy myth as in this deeply romantic painting. It shows Canada's widely celebrated heroine Laura Secord, accompanied by Indian guides, on her way to warn British officers that U.S. troops are approaching.

The Battle of Tippecanoe is often considered part of the War of 1812 even though it took place months before the war was officially declared. Fought in the wilds of the Northwest, it pitted Native warriors against frontiersmen led by William Henry Harrison, shown here on a white charger. The battle was far from the glorious American victory this Currier & Ives illustration suggests.

I

Northwest Theater

WAR IN THE WILDERNESS

DURING THE EARLY NINETEENTH CENTURY, the western Great Lakes region, known to most Americans then as the "Old Northwest," was exceedingly remote. To reach Fort Detroit at the western end of Lake Erie from the population centers along the East Coast required a difficult journey of several weeks. If something important happened in the East—for instance, a declaration of war—the pioneers and territorial officials of the Northwest might not hear about it for more than a month.

Covered by dense forests and open prairies seldom broken by roads or settlements, the Northwest was in several senses a frontier. The border between the British province of Upper Canada—the present day Province of Ontario—and the Indiana Territory of the United States ran through it. So, too, did the indistinct and ever-shifting line of demarcation between recently established farms and communities and the steadily retreating western wilderness. Also cutting through it—and even less firmly fixed—was the boundary between the lands held by white settlers and those claimed by various Indian peoples.

This vast expanse of continental heartland offered fertile soils, plentiful game, abundant timber, and the promise of mineral wealth. These rich lands and resources had long since begun to attract settlers of European decent who pressed westward across the Allegheny Mountains and down the great chain of lakes. Inevitably, land-hungry pioneers bumped up against Native American tribes, many of which had earlier retreated from the East and were not prepared to make them welcome.

Native American leaders, such as the great Shawnee warrior Tecumseh, rose up and counseled their peoples to resist the tide of white intruders. They made it clear to the newcomers that their warriors would fight and die, if necessary, to preserve the Indian way of life. During their famous parlay at Vincennes, Tecumseh had said as much to William Henry Harrison, Governor of the Indiana Territory. "My brother," Tecumseh told Harrison, "I do not see how we can remain at peace with you."

In essence, a state of war had existed in the Northwest for months—if not years—prior to the opening of hostilities between the United States and Britain. Once the War of 1812 was officially underway, the British in Upper Canada found ready allies among the Indians, who aided them by keeping the American frontier in a constant state of turmoil. Native American

The War of 1812 dawned in the Northwest, where frontier militia fought Native American warriors and untested U.S. troops confronted better prepared British regulars at Mackinac Island, Detroit, and elsewhere.

warriors would also provide Britain's small western armies with the margin of victory in several important battles, most notably at Fort Detroit, Fort Dearborn, and the Raisin River. In return, the British provided the Indians with weapons, food, and supplies.

Despite their problems with the Indians, the Americans began the war in the Northwest with what appeared to be several major advantages. Most significant of these was population. Overall, Americans outnumbered Canadians by a margin of perhaps fourteen to one, but in the Northwest, the U.S. population advantage was even greater. In fact, many of the settlers in the western portions of Upper Canada had migrated there from the United States, which made their loyalty to the crown questionable at best. Because of the war with the Indians, the United States had veteran regulars and militia in the Northwest and held a number of important strong points such as Fort Detroit and Fort Mackinac. And since it was the Americans who had declared war, their forces had—or ought to have had—the initiative. As we shall see, however, none of these advantages would prove decisive.

Maintaining forces along the northwestern frontier was a daunting task for both sides. Most supplies had to be brought in by boat using the lakes and rivers as liquid highways. Consequently, control of the lakes would provide the key to victory in the northwestern theater. By seizing control of the waterways in the Battle of the Great Lakes on September 10, 1813, the United States finally gained the upper hand. This crucial edge would enable the Americans to hold onto their northwestern territories, but not, as things turned out, to conquer Upper Canada.

TIPPECANOE BATTLEFIELD
Lafayette, Indiana

A SOARING OBELISK NOW MARKS THE SITE of what some historians consider the first battle of the War of 1812. However, the fighting here took place more than seven months before the U.S. Congress voted a formal declaration of war. In the fall of 1811, Governor William Henry Harrison and an army of about 1,100 frontier militiamen and U.S. regulars advanced on Prophetstown, the epicenter of Tecumseh's fledgling tribal confederacy. On the evening of November 6, Harrison and his troops pitched camp only about 2 miles from their objective.

To guard against a preemptive Indian attack, Harrison selected a campsite located on a blade-like peninsula of high ground enclosed on three sides by a marshy prairie. He ordered his troops to keep their weapons close beside them as they slept. Before bedding down for the night, his men loaded their guns and fixed bayonets. These would prove to have been wise precautions for in nearby Prophetstown hundreds of Shawnee, Ottawa, Huron, Kickapoo, Chippawa, and Pottawatomi warriors were dancing and working themselves into a frenzy.

BATTLE OF TIPPECANOE—WHERE JO DAVIESS FELL.

The Northwest was a frontier in every sense of the word, and the fighting that took place there was often desperate and brutal. When Native Americans met American frontiersmen in battle, mercy was seldom asked and even more rarely granted.

On his way south to seek support among the Creeks for his confederacy, Tecumseh was not in Prophetstown at the time. However, his brother Tenskwatawa, known to his followers as the Prophet, was present, and he told the warriors that they could attack their enemies without fear. His prayers would make them invulnerable to the soldiers' bullets, or so he insisted.

About two hours before dawn on November 7, a force of roughly 700 warriors descended on Harrison's camp from the north, let out a terrifying whoop, and attacked. Readers today may imagine what happened next as a clash of knives, tomahawks, bayonets, and rifle butts, but much of the fighting did not take this form. Instead, the Battle of Tippecanoe was mostly fought with muskets and rifles fired from the cover of fallen tree trunks. For more than two hours the flash of igniting black powder lit up the night while soldiers and warriors fell in twos and threes. Finally, sometime after sunrise, the superior equipment and discipline of Harrison's troops began to tell, and the Prophet's surviving braves slipped away into the forest.

The battle had been costly, with each side suffering about 200 killed and wounded. But Harrison and his army remained in possession of the battlefield. Harrison's men spent the remainder of the day tending to their wounded and reorganizing units. Then, on the following morning, they pushed on to Prophetstown, which by that time had been abandoned. There the soldiers found a number of muskets and other weapons that appeared to have been supplied by the British. Later this discovery would be put forward as evidence that British agents were encouraging western tribes to attack American settlements.

Before leaving the area, Harrison ordered the village burned. Every home and shed went up in flames, including thousands of bushels of stored beans and corn. In a final act of wanton desecration, his men uncovered the graves of Indian dead and dumped the bodies on the ground to rot and be torn apart by animals.

Afterward, Harrison and his army beat a hasty retreat toward the east, a clear indication that the Battle of Tippecanoe had not been an unqualified victory. But neither was it a defeat. Although he didn't know it at the time, Harrison had achieved at least one of his primary goals. His Indian country campaign had fatally disrupted Tecumseh's fledgling confederacy.

It had also discredited Tenskwatawa in the eyes of his own people. The Prophet's prayers had not stopped the soldiers' bullets. Having watched their friends gunned down by the whites, the warriors later turned on the Prophet and threatened to kill him. Eventually, the shaman was driven into exile when he was denounced even by his own brother, Tecumseh.

Otherwise, the Battle of Tippecanoe settled nothing. Instead, it proved to have been the opening salvo of a war that was just beginning. Harrison's assault on Prophetstown left behind such a harvest of bitterness that Native American peoples in the Great Lakes region would have no real choice but to side with the British in the coming War of 1812. Tecumseh gave voice to that bitterness when he returned to the area a few months after the battle.

"Governor Harrison made war on my people in my absence," he said. "On my return I found great destruction and havoc—the fruits of our labor destroyed, the bodies of my friends laying in the dust, and our village burnt to the ground by the Big Knives."

WHAT YOU'LL SEE TODAY

LOCATED OFF STATE ROUTE 225 in Indiana's Tippecanoe County, the Tippecanoe Battlefield Park extends over approximately 100 acres of grassy meadow and woodland. The battlefield itself is much smaller in extent and can be reached by way of scenic trails. Important features of this National Historic Landmark are interpreted by way of plaques. A museum operated by the Tippecanoe County Historical Association helps put it all in perspective.

Perhaps the most prominent feature of the park is a soaring obelisk placed here in 1908 as a memorial to those who died in the battle. On one side of the obelisk stands a full-sized statue of William Henry Harrison. Although depicted here in cold, colorless marble, he nonetheless appears resplendent in his peaked hat and military regalia.

About a mile east of the battlefield is Prophetstown State Park, which preserves the site of Tecumseh's tribal confederacy capital. Nothing remains of the original village, although visitors can see replicas of the medicine lodge and council house. The park also features a working prairie farm famed for its draft horses.

FORT ST. JOSEPH
St. Joseph Island, Ontario

LAKES HURON AND MICHIGAN ARE LINKED to one another by way of the narrow Straits of Mackinac which separate what is known today as the Upper and Lower Michigan Peninsulas. Less than 50 miles to the east of the straits, the St. Mary's River dumps the overflow from mighty Lake Superior into Lake Huron. The British had once dominated this strategic intersection of waterways with their fort on Mackinac Island at the eastern end of the straits. However, under the terms of Jay's Treaty, signed in 1794, they were forced to turn this important strongpoint over to the Americans. Afterward, the British established a new fort in Upper Canada on St. Joseph's Island near the mouth of the St. Mary's.

During the summer of 1812, Fort St. Joseph was under the command of an enterprising young British Army captain named Charles Roberts. When General Isaac Brock, the governor of Upper Canada, heard that war had been declared, he sent canoes hurrying westward to notify various isolated British outposts such as Fort St. Joseph. Having received this vital intelligence, Captain Roberts quickly organized an assault on Fort Mackinac.

Located near the intersections of three giant lakes, Mackinac Island could hardly have been more strategically positioned. Unfortunately for the Americans, they would lose the island fortress in one of the war's very first engagements.

On July 16, 1812, about 200 British regulars and militia set out for Mackinac Island in small boats accompanied by several hundred Indians in war canoes. Early the next morning, Roberts' troops and allied warriors landed on Mackinac Island, where they caught the small American garrison completely by surprise. Having thus captured the more strategically placed Fort Mackinac, the British largely abandoned Fort St. Joseph. American forces burned what remained of the fort during the summer of 1814.

WHAT YOU'LL SEE TODAY

NOW A NATIONAL HISTORIC SITE operated by Parks Canada, Fort St. Joseph is located at the southern end of Ontario's St. Joseph Island. The island is accessible via a causeway and Route 548 which turns off Trans Canada Highway 17 about 28 miles (45 kilometers) southeast of Sault Ste. Marie. Visitors can tour ruins of the fort and learn much about the fascinating history of this place from displays in the visitor center. Relatively undeveloped, St. Joseph Island offers an abundance of beautiful vistas and delights for nature lovers including moose, deer, beaver, and nesting eagles. Because it is remote, Fort St. Joseph receives fewer visitors than many of Canada's better known War of 1812 sites. It is nonetheless important because it was from here that British forces launched one of the first and most successful maneuvers of the conflict.

FORT MACKINAC
Mackinac Island, Michigan

LIEUTENANT PORTER HANKS RECEIVED WHAT WAS probably the surprise of his life on the morning of July 17, 1812 when he awoke and saw a cannon pointing toward him from a hill overlooking Fort Mackinac. Arrayed around the fort and its garrison of 57 U.S. regulars was a sizeable force of Canadian militia and British regulars bolstered by an even larger Native American war party. Until that moment, Hanks had been completely unaware that his country was at war. By some bizarre oversight, no one had bothered to inform him.

At 10 a.m. that same morning, Hanks received a stern warning from Captain Charles Roberts, the British officer leading the forces besieging the fort: Hanks must surrender the fort immediately or face the consequences. As commander of this remote but strategically vital frontier outpost, Hanks was faced with a very painful decision. Ill-prepared for an attack and outflanked by the enemy artillery, he could see that resistance was futile. So, he ordered his men to lay down their arms. According to the terms of the surrender, Hanks and the other American troops at Fort Mackinac were set free on parole, meaning that they promised not to fight again so long as the United States and Britain remained at war.

American military and political leaders were thunderstruck when they learned the British had taken Fort Mackinac. Without the firing of a single shot, the United States had lost a critically important military post that some saw as the key to the entire midcontinent. The British and Canadians, on the other hand, were greatly encouraged. In addition to giving them control over the Straits of Mackinac, this early victory made it much easier to recruit Native American allies. The capture of Fort Mackinac considerably increased the likelihood that they could prevent the Americans from seizing Upper Canada.

At the time of the War of 1812, the western Great Lakes region was exceedingly remote. This painting shows Mackinac Island as it may have appeared before the British attacked during the early weeks of the conflict. The American troops there were not even aware that war had been declared.

Following the decisive American naval victory in the Battle of the Great Lakes, U.S. forces attempted to retake the post, which the British had renamed Fort George. On July 26, 1814 a U.S. fleet consisting of three brigs and two schooners approached Mackinac Island and placed it under siege. A week later the fleet put ashore about 750 regulars, militia, and marines who attempted to march on Fort George from the rear. A smaller British force of about 150 regulars and militia bolstered by some 350 Menominee Indian warriors, confronted the Americans well to the north of the fort. Deployed in a forest along the edge of a strip of cleared farmland, the British under Lieutenant Colonel Robert McDouall had excellent cover. The Americans, led by Lieutenant Colonel George Croghan, tried several times to outflank his enemy's strong position but without success. Unable to dislodge the British, Croghan ordered his men back to their ships.

WHAT YOU'LL SEE TODAY

RETURNED TO THE UNITED STATES following the War of 1812, Mackinac Island is now a popular summertime tourist destination. Accessible by swift ferry from St. Ignace on the Upper Michigan Peninsula and Mackinac City on the Lower Peninsula, the island is known for its elegant Grand Hotel, quaint streets, maple fudge, and horse-drawn transportation—motorized vehicles are not allowed here. Most structures date from the late nineteenth and early twentieth centuries, and visitors get the feeling they have been transported back in time. At Fort Mackinac, they may feel they have traveled all the way back to 1812.

Guides in early-nineteenth-century dress welcome visitors to the fort, which has been painstakingly restored so that it looks much as it did during the war. Within the fort's stone palisades overlooking the straits are fourteen of its original buildings. During the tourist season, historic interpreters in period military uniforms drill on the fortress parade ground and an antique, six-pounder cannon is fired several times a day. Elsewhere on the island, plaques mark the sites of the British landing in 1812, the Battle of Mackinac Island in 1814, and Fort Holmes, which was named for Major Andrew Hunter Holmes, an American officer killed in the fighting here.

Supply Strategy in the Northwest

Although roads in the Northwest were either primitive or nonexistence, the Americans there were usually able to supply their troops by land. The watery and broken geography of Canada made this much more difficult for the British. Amherstburg and other remote British outposts relied heavily on food, clothing, arms, and other supplies shipped in by way of Lake Erie. Perry's defeat and capture of Barclay's fleet at the Battle of Lake Erie severed this essential link and left British forces in a near hopeless position in the Northwest.

FORT MALDEN

Amherstburg, Ontario

ORIGINALLY CALLED FORT AMHERSTBURG but later known as Fort Malden, this frontier outpost was established in 1796. Strategically located near the place where the Detroit River empties into Lake Erie, the earth-and-wood fortress served as headquarters for British land and naval forces in the western Great Lakes. Intended to give the British more leverage in dealing with the Americans, the fort also provided a convenient place to meet with Native American war chiefs and forge alliances with western tribes. It was here that General Isaac Brock met Tecumseh in August of 1812 and from here that he launched his successful attack on Fort Detroit, then the most important U.S. military asset in the Northwest.

During the first year of the war, the docks and naval facilities at Amherstburg enabled the British to dominate Lake Erie. From the shipyards here they launched several of the key ships in their western Great Lakes fleet, including the *General Hunter, Queen Charlotte, Lady Provost,* and *Detroit*. However, these and other vessels were defeated and captured by Commodore Perry's fleet at the Battle of Lake Erie in September 1813. This calamitous reversal cut off supplies from the east and made the post vulnerable to attack from the lake. Consequently, British forces burned the fort and nearby naval facilities and retreated eastward. In early October, the Army of General William Henry Harrison caught up with and defeated them at the Battle of the Thames.

The U.S. Plan for Invasion of Canada

The United States entered the War of 1812 with no clear idea of how to proceed. The American plan, such as it was, involved a three-prong invasion of Canada. Using Fort Detroit as a staging area, one army would invade Upper Canada from the west. A second army would cross the Niagara River and seize the provincial capital at York, while a third army would sweep northward toward the St. Lawrence River and Montreal. All three invasion efforts were poorly organized and even more poorly led. The western and central campaigns ended disastrously while the planned advance into the valley of the St. Lawrence never really materialized.

Isaac Brock on the Detroit Frontier

A man of extraordinary vision and leadership ability, General Isaac Brock had anticipated trouble with the Americans. When war was declared, Brock moved much faster and with greater clarity of purpose than his counterparts below the border. Having ordered his forces at Fort St. Joseph to seize nearby Fort Mackinac, Brock hurried westward to Fort Malden with 300 well-trained British regulars. After an American campaign aimed at capturing Fort Malden failed for lack of siege cannon and effective leadership, Brock responded by attacking Fort Detroit. Although heavily outnumbered, Brock employed a combination of ruthless bravado and deception to persuade his enemies to surrender.

In his confrontation with Hull at Fort Detroit, Brock was aided by a key piece of intelligence. Several weeks before his attack on Detroit, Brock's men had captured the *Cuyahoga,* an American supply vessel. Onboard were General Hull's official papers, which Brock was later able to read. Consequently, he knew all of Hull's plans as well as the strength and disposition of American forces along the Northwest frontier.

The Americans remained in control of Amherstburg and the Detroit River region until the end of the war. During this time they attempted to rebuild the fort, but the project was never completed. The Fort Malden seen today was built after the war on the ruins of the original fortifications.

WHAT YOU'LL SEE TODAY

ONE OF CANADA'S MANY WELL-MAINTAINED National Historic Sites, Fort Malden is located in Amherstburg about 30 miles (45 kilometers) south of Windsor and the Detroit River bridges. The site includes an interpretive center with displays focusing on the War of 1812 as well as restored earthworks

General Isaac Brock believed that only speedy offensive action could save Upper Canada from the Americans.

and buildings. Guides dressed in period military uniforms help visitors understand the importance of the fort and what life was like for soldiers stationed here. Also in Amherstburg is the original Provincial Marine Commissariat, which is located in King's Navy Yard Park.

BATTLE OF BROWNSTONE
Gibraltar, Michigan

TO LEAD THE AMERICAN ARMY IN THE NORTHWEST, officials in Washington turned to William Hull, governor of the Michigan Territory and a respected veteran of the Revolutionary War. At age fifty-eight, Hull was probably far too old for a frontier command, and he was in ill health. Even so, Hull gathered approximately 2,000 troops at Fort Detroit and, as ordered, attempted to invade Canada. On July 12, 1812 Hull crossed the Detroit River intending to march on Fort Malden. However, he was unable to transport the cannon he needed to reduce the British fortifications and, startled by the news that Fort Mackinac had fallen, soon withdrew to the seeming safety of Detroit.

Hull withdrew in part because the supply lines he needed to keep his army fed, clothed, and armed were far from secure. Tecumseh and his warriors mercilessly harassed any supply column that attempted to reach the Americans. In a small but nonetheless important skirmish fought on August 4, 1812 near the village of Brownstone, Tecumseh and two dozen warriors ambushed a detachment of about 200 American troops trying to break through to a supply column that had tried but failed to reach Hull's army. Thinking they were greatly outnumbered by the Indians, the Americans turned back. Five days later, on August 9, a larger column of U.S. soldiers defeated a mixed force of British regulars, Canadian militia, and Native American warriors near an Indian village called Monguagon. Although the Americans won the Battle of Monguagon, they failed to reopen the vital supply line to Ohio and a week later Hull surrendered Fort Detroit.

Fort Detroit was the most important U.S. military post in the Northwest. Its loss to a mixed force of British regulars and Indian warriors on August 16, 1812 was a stunning blow to the American war effort.

WHAT YOU'LL SEE TODAY

ABOUT 15 MILES SOUTH OF DETROIT in the town of Gibraltar, Michigan, a Michigan State Plaque marks the site of the Battle of Brownstone. The plaque is located on Gibraltar Road near Parson's Elementary School. A historical marker describing the Battle of Monguagon is located in Elizabeth Park in the riverside Detroit suburb of Trenton.

FORT DETROIT
Detroit, Michigan

CONSISTING OF ABOUT 150 HOUSES surrounded by a stockade, Detroit was more a rough-and-tumble frontier town than a secure military fortress. It proved difficult to defend, when in the middle of August General Isaac Brock turned the tables on Hull, crossed the Detroit River, and laid siege to the place. Brock's siege was, in fact, a colossal bluff. His invasion force of little more than 1,000 regulars, Canadian militia, and Native American warriors were significantly outnumbered by the Fort Detroit garrison. Nonetheless, Brock demanded that Hull surrender.

"I require of you the immediate surrender of Fort Detroit," he said to Hull in a note delivered under a flag of truce. "It is far from my intention to join in a war of extermination; but you must be aware that the numerous body of Indians who have attached themselves to my troops will be beyond my control the moment the contest commences."

All the while, Brock had his men and Tecumseh's warriors make as much noise as possible. It appeared to Hull, who was ill and terrified of an Indian massacre, that he was vastly outnumbered. Even worse, British cannon balls were already blasting through the fort's wooden stockade to maim and kill the soldiers and civilians huddled within. Ironically, one of the first rounds fired at the fort decapitated Lieutenant Porter Hanks who had surrendered Fort Mackinac only a few weeks earlier. Confused and dispirited, Hull agreed to surrender.

Old, ill, and befuddled, General William Hull surrendered Fort Detroit after a siege of only two days.

This victory gave the British control of the Michigan frontier for the better part of a year. A considerable number of cannon and more than 2,000 muskets were captured and used to arm Canadian militia units. News of the surrender convinced more Native American tribes to side with the British with the result that raids on American frontier settlements and outposts increased dramatically.

The British held Fort Detroit for little more than a year before abandoning it in the face of an American counteroffensive at the end of September 1813. The mostly bloodless recapture was made possible by the success of Commodore Perry at the Battle of Lake Erie. Renamed Fort Shelby, the fortress remained in American hands for the rest of the war.

WHAT YOU'LL SEE TODAY

DURING THE WAR OF 1812, Forts Detroit and Shelby stood at the edge of a wilderness that has long since vanished. Today, the original site of the outpost is buried beneath multiple layers of concrete. A plaque at Fort and Shelby Streets in downtown Detroit marks the approximate position of the fort, which stood not far from what are today the Detroit Visitor Center, the Renaissance Center, and Tigers Stadium. Standing in the midst of urban Detroit and reading this plaque puts the War of 1812 into a full 200 years of perspective. Clearly, the soldiers and warriors who fought and died here were fighting for a future they could never have imagined.

Most of the Americans and others who lost their lives at Fort Detroit were not cut down by bullets but rather by cold, hunger, and disease. Many were buried in a common grave, its location indicated by a marker at the corner of Detroit's Washington and Michigan Avenues. Standing in a nearby median is a statue of General Alexander Macomb, who was born at Detroit in 1782. In 1814 Macomb commanded the American troops who halted a major British invasion force at Plattsburgh, New York.

Across the Detroit River in Windsor, Ontario, is the Francois Baby House used by General Hull as a headquarters during his brief invasion of Canada. Now a National Historic Site of Canada, the house at 221 Mill Street serves as the current home of Windsor Community Museum. A plaque off Riverside Drive indicates the landing site of Hull's troops.

FORT DEARBORN MASSACRE
Chicago, Illinois

THE EARLY MONTHS OF THE WAR went badly for the Americans throughout the Northwest. One of the worst and most tragic setbacks took place in mid-August near Fort Dearborn, which stood along the southwestern shores of Lake Michigan. Although the fort had been under virtual siege by hostile Indians since April, it was strongly built and might have held out much longer. After the fall of Fort Mackinac, however, General Hull feared the worst for small outposts like Dearborn. Consequently, he sent a dispatch from Detroit ordering Captain Nathan Heald and his 54-man garrison to abandon the fort and retreat southward.

On August 15, 1812, Heald and his men marched out of Fort Dearborn accompanied by about forty civilians, most of them women and children. Little more than a mile from the fort, near a stretch of rolling dunes beside the lake, they were set upon by a large Indian war party. Fifty-two of the Fort Dearborn refugees were killed in the attack and the rest taken prisoner. British agents later purchased the captives and immediately set them free. The warriors burned Fort Dearborn, and the post was not reoccupied by U.S. forces until after the war.

Indian warriors often executed enemies captured in battle. Massacres such as the one at Fort Dearborn struck fear into the hearts of American settlers along the frontier. The illustration above shows warriors killing prisoners captured near Frenchtown.

WHAT YOU'LL SEE TODAY

THE SKYSCRAPERS OF DOWNTOWN Chicago now tower above the original site of Fort Dearborn. The outline of the stockade is indicated by bronze markers laid into the concrete of the sidewalk on the south side of the Chicago River near the Michigan Avenue Bridge. A sculpture and inscription on the bridge commemorate the massacre as does a small park at 18th Street and Calumet Avenue near the spot where the killings took place.

RIVER RAISIN BATTLEFIELD
Monroe, Michigan

EARLY IN 1813 AMERICAN FORCES under General William Henry Harrison attempted to push the British back into Canada and retake Detroit. To accomplish this and to shore up U.S. defenses in the Northwest, Harrison assembled an army of several thousand men. Approximately 1,300 of these were placed under the command of General James Winchester, who, without clear orders from Harrison, marched his men northward into present-day Michigan. Lacking food and fodder for their horses, Winchester's troops were forced to halt at Frenchtown, a small settlement on the River Raisin.

On January 22, 1813 the American camp at Frenchtown was attacked by a smaller British force that included about 500 British regulars and Canadian militia accompanied by some 600 Indians led by Tecumseh. Caught completely by surprise, Winchester's troops were initially panicked but soon managed to form a makeshift defensive line. Unfortunately for the Americans, Tecumseh's warriors fell then upon their right flank, pushing it back toward the river. Captured in the ensuing rout, Winchester then ordered his men on the left flank to surrender. Nearly 400 Americans were killed, with another 500 taken prisoner. Some of the prisoners were later massacred by the Indians. The defeat at Frenchtown and the killings that followed gave rise to the slogan "Remember the Raisin" that became a popular rallying cry among American fighting men in the Northwest.

WHAT YOU'LL SEE TODAY

A STONE MEMORIAL DEDICATED to American troops killed in the battle is located on Monroe Street just south of downtown Monroe, Michigan. Nearby, a second monument pays tribute to the many Kentucky riflemen who fell in the battle. Its inscription is entitled: MICHIGAN'S TRIBUTE TO KENTUCKY. Congress has passed legislation designating the site of the battle as the River Raisin National Battlefield Park.

FORT MEIGS
Perrysburg, Ohio

FOLLOWING THE DISASTER AT THE RIVER RAISIN, Harrison and his remaining forces fell back toward Ohio where they established fortifications on the south bank of the Maumee River near the Miami Rapids. Harrison named this new base of operations Fort Meigs after Ohio Governor R.J. Meigs. Then he hurried off to Cincinnati to raise additional troops for another attempt to invade Canada.

For greater effect, War of 1812 infantry units often fired their rifles and muskets in massive volleys. Here re-enactors at Fort Meigs participate in a volley fire exercise.

Meanwhile, in Upper Canada, British General Henry Proctor contemplated an invasion of his own. Proctor felt that a well-timed spoiling attack on U.S. military posts south of Lake Erie might forestall any new American offensives aimed at Detroit or Amherstburg. At first Proctor considered an assault on Presque Isle where the Americans were building a fleet intended to seize control of the western lakes. However, Proctor felt he had insufficient forces for a successful raid on the Presque Isle shipyards and opted instead for an attack on Fort Meigs.

In late April 1813, a British fleet arrived at the mouth of the Maumee and put ashore 1,000 regulars and Canadian militia. Supported by some 1,200 warriors under Tecumseh, these troops marched up the river hauling with them eleven powerful cannon. Once they arrived in front of Fort Meigs, Proctor ordered his men to establish a pair of batteries, one on each side of the river. On May 1, the British artillery opened fire on the fort.

By this time, Harrison had returned to Fort Meigs with reinforcements. Proctor's siege forces were now steadfastly opposed by 1,100 determined American defenders. Harrison rallied them with stirring language. "Can the citizens of a free country think of submitting

American infantrymen were generally not as well trained or effective in open-field combat as their British opponents. In this photograph, however, U.S. re-enactors are shown delivering what surely would have been a devastating volley.

Tecumseh intervenes to prevent the slaughter of American prisoners captured during the first siege of Fort Meigs. This incident greatly enhanced his reputation as a respected—and humane—leader.

to an army composed of mercenary soldiers, reluctant Canadians, goaded to the field by the bayonet, and of wretched naked savages?" he asked them. "To your posts then fellow citizens, and remember that the eyes of your country are upon you."

It quickly became obvious to Proctor that Fort Meigs would not be as easily captured as he had hoped. Encompassing an area of nearly ten acres, its wooden walls were fifteen feet high and reinforced by eight substantial blockhouses. The river protected the north side of the fort while steep ravines made it difficult to approach from other directions. What was worse, a relief force of 1,200 Kentucky militiamen under General Green Clay was rapidly approaching from the south.

When Clay arrived on May 5, Harrison ordered him to send 800 of his Kentuckians across the Maumee to attack the British battery on the north side of the river. This detachment commanded by Colonel William Dudley managed to capture the battery but was soon overwhelmed by a combined British and Indian counterattack. More than 300 of Dudley's men were killed or wounded and most of the remainder captured.

Despite this victory, Proctor was unable to maintain the siege. Most of his artillery rounds were plunging harmlessly into a twelve-foot high earthen embankment that Harrison's men had hurriedly constructed. Additional American reinforcements were closing in on the Maumee while increasing numbers of Proctor's Indian allies were tiring of the siege and drifting away into the forest. On May 9 Proctor lifted the siege and returned with his men to Canada.

In late July, Proctor and Tecumseh tried once again to take Fort Meigs but were no more successful than they had been three months earlier. Hoping to convince the Americans that a relief column was under attack, Tecumseh and his warriors attempted to draw the garrison out the fort by staging a noisy mock battle in the nearby forest.

Colonel Clay, who was in command of the fort at the time, was not deceived, and Tecumseh's ruse failed. Soon afterward Proctor called off the siege. Later, when Harrison decided to shift his forces elsewhere, he ordered the fort destroyed to make sure this seeming indestructible place never fell into enemy hands.

Although not original structures, the carefully reconstructed blockhouse and stockade at Fort Meigs in Ohio enable park visitors to envision the fort as it may have appeared 200 years ago.

WHAT YOU'LL SEE TODAY

IN 1974 FORT MEIGS WAS REBUILT on its original site by the Ohio Historical Society, which operates it as a public education and recreation facility. The log-and-earthen structure is part of Fort Meigs State Memorial Park located in Perrysburg a few miles southwest of Toledo. The 65-arce park and museum complex includes stockades, blockhouses, exhibits, classrooms, and a gift shop.

PRESQUE ISLE SHIPYARD
Erie, Pennsylvania

DURING THE FIRST YEAR OF THE WAR OF 1812, the British enjoyed naval superiority on the Great Lakes, and this gave them a considerable advantage in the western theaters of the conflict. Because it linked the more settled East with the western territories, Erie was particularly strategic, and the British Provincial Marine dominated it with half a dozen well-constructed fighting ships. These included the *Queen Charlotte, Hunter, Provost, Nancy, Caledonia,* and *Detroit,* which together mounted more than seventy cannon. The United States, on the other hand, had no warships worthy of mention to counter this powerful fleet.

Military officials in the United States sought to correct the imbalance of naval strength on the lakes by building a fleet capable of challenging the British. An experienced lake mariner, U.S. Navy sailing master Daniel Dobbins was put in charge of this daunting task. For a shipyard, Dobbins selected Presque Isle, a sandy fishhook peninsula near Erie, Pennsylvania. Presque Isle offered a calm, protected harbor and an abundance of stout oak in nearby forests to provide materials for ribs and planking. Late in 1812, Dobbins gathered the best workmen he could find—few had any experience building large vessels—and set them to work.

Britain's General Proctor knew full well what the Americans were attempting at Presque Isle and briefly considered an attack on the shipyard. Believing that he lacked the men, guns, and supplies necessary for the enterprise, he gave up on the idea. Had he decided otherwise and managed to destroy the American naval facilities at Presque Isle, the war in the western Great Lakes region might have taken a very different course.

Oliver Hazard Perry was only twenty-eight when he led the American fleet to victory at the decisive Battle of Lake Erie.

As it was, without interference from the British, the Americans were able to launch one warship after another throughout the spring and early summer of 1813. By August of that year, the Presque Isle shipyard had completed the gunboats *Ariel, Porcupine, Tigress,* and *Scorpion* and a pair of twenty-gun brigs, the *Lawrence* and *Niagara*. Three converted merchant vessels and a small brig captured from the British were later added to the American fleet, which in September was able to outmaneuver and outgun the British at the pivotal Battle of Lake Erie.

Commodore Oliver Hazard Perry commanded the victorious U.S. flotilla in that battle and later brought his ships back to winter at Presque Isle. The winter of 1813-1814 proved especially severe, and more than a few of Perry's sailors died of exposure, privation, and disease. In memory of that terrible time, the body of water partially enclosed by the Presque Isle Peninsula was afterward widely known as Misery Bay.

WHAT YOU'LL SEE TODAY

NOTHING REMAINS OF THE SHIPYARD where inexperienced shipwrights built most of the vessels that would comprise the U.S. Lake Erie fleet. However, in Presque Isle State Park there is a 100-foot stone monument dedicated Commodore Perry and to those who died serving with him on the Great Lakes. Known primarily for its beaches, game fishing, and nature trails, Presque Isle State Park can be reached from Erie via Pennsylvania 832 or by water from Presque Isle (Misery) Bay.

The Erie Maritime Museum on the Erie waterfront offers informative displays on the War of 1812 and the part played in it by the Presque Isle shipyard and naval base. Also of interest is the Flagship Niagara, a replica of the U.S. brig that fought at the Battle of Lake Erie. Visitors can book summertime cruises on this authentically reconstructed vessel.

PERRY VICTORY MONUMENT

South Bass Island, Ohio

POLITICAL AND MILITARY LEADERS in the United States knew that to win the war in the Northwest they must seize control of Lake Erie. To accomplish this, Commodore Perry assembled a fleet of brigs and gunboats at Presque Isle. During July, a British flotilla bottled up Perry's fleet by establishing a blockade of the Presque Isle harbor. By the end of the month, however, supply shortages forced the British warships to return to their base at Amherstburg. Perry and his men were then able to work their vessels over the treacherous bar at the entrance to Presque Isle Bay and into the open waters of Lake Erie. Both sides now understood only too well that a major confrontation between the opposing fleets was inevitable.

For more than a month, the British fleet led by Commander Robert Heriot Barclay, a Trafalgar veteran, avoided battle. Now outnumbered, if not outgunned, by the Americans,

Under intense fire from the British, Perry calmly transfers his flag from the crippled Lawrence. *Once safely aboard the nearby 20-gun brig* Niagara, *Perry led a renewed American assault that soon forced the British fleet to surrender.*

CAPT. ROBERT H. BARCLAY, 1814.
In Uniform of Period.

The British fleet on Lake Erie was commanded by Robert Heriot Barclay, a Trafalgar veteran even younger than Perry.

Barclay awaited completion of the 490-ton, nineteen-gun *Detroit*. When the *Detroit* was finally ready for action, Barclay set sail from Amherstburg heading directly toward the recently established American naval base at Put-in-Bay on Ohio's South Bass Island. Barclay had no choice but to force a fight since Perry's presence in the lake had cut off supplies to British forces at Amhersburg and Detroit.

On the morning of September 10, Perry's lookouts sighted the sails of Barclay's ships, and the American fleet hurried out into the lake to meet them. For a while the two fleets maneuvered, each of them seeking the weather gauge, that is, the advantage of having the wind at their backs. This was especially important for Perry since his heavier cannon had a shorter effective range than the so-called long cannon on the British ships. To win the battle, Perry knew he had to move in close until he was literally within shouting range of his enemies.

By 11:45 a.m. the British and American flotillas were arrayed in two lines directly opposite one another, and the opening shots of the battle were fired. The heaviest fire, from the long cannons of the British, fell on Perry's flagship, the *Lawrence*. Her sister ship, the *Niagara*, had fallen too far behind to help, and the *Lawrence* was soon smashed to splinters by fire from the entire British fleet. The *Lawrence* eventually moved in close enough to deliver telling blows with her heavy cannon, but four out of every five members of her crew were either killed or wounded in the resulting melee.

The *Lawrence* had been named in honor of Captain James Lawrence who had been killed when his frigate *Chesapeake* was defeated by the British frigate *Shannon* off the coast of Massachusetts. The *Lawrence* flew from her mast a pennant bearing Captain Lawrence's dying words: "Don't give up the ship." But when the last operable cannon on the *Lawrence* finally fell silent, that is exactly what Perry did. Perry stepped into an open boat and rowed across to the *Niagara,* which by that time was close enough to render assistance.

The *Lawrence* then surrendered to the British, but Captain Barclay and his men had little cause to celebrate their apparent victory. The British ships had taken terrible punishment, their decks were awash in blood, and Barclay himself was seriously wounded. Perhaps even worse, the two largest British vessels, *Queen Charlotte* and *Detroit,* had been all but put out of action when they collided with one another while attempting to change course.

Once onboard the *Niagara,* Perry ordered his remaining ships to renew their attack, and they soon turned the tide of the battle. By 3 p.m. all six of Barclay's ships had been forced to strike their colors. Later that same day Perry wrote his now famous message to General Harrison who waited anxiously on shore for word of the outcome. On the back of a used envelope, Perry scrawled: "We have met the enemy and they are ours. Two ships, two brigs, one schooner, and one sloop."

Perry's victory in the Battle of Lake Erie placed British forces in the western Great Lakes region in an untenable position. Cut off from reinforcements and supplies that were

A dignified procession of small boats ferry the dead ashore after the Battle of Lake Erie. The victorious American sailors showed great respect for their fallen foes and buried them with honors.

normally shipped in by way of the lake, Fort Detroit, Fort Malden, and the naval facilities at Amherstburg were now hopelessly vulnerable to attack. With the help of Perry's now much enlarged fleet, General Harrison soon captured all three, and the British war effort in the Northwest Theater never fully recovered from Barclay's defeat.

WHAT YOU'LL SEE TODAY

THE BATTLE OF LAKE ERIE took place out on the open water where, of course, there is nothing to see today but waves. Perhaps the most dramatic way to commemorate the battle is to visit Perry's Victory and International Peace Memorial located near Put-in-Bay on South Bass Island. The island and the memorial are accessible by ferry from Port Clinton, Ohio. The memorial takes the form of a giant Doric column more than 350 feet tall, and it has a flashing beacon at the top which enables it to serve as a lighthouse. Visitors are allowed to climb to the top of the memorial where an observation deck provides an astounding view of open blue water and distant dark green shoreline. From the considerable height of the platform—roughly equal to that of a thirty-story building—it is possible to look westward and imagine the fateful collision of the American and British fleets two centuries ago. A well-designed visitor center not far from the base of the memorial tells the complete story of the battle.

Interestingly enough, when it was completed in 1915, the memorial was intended not so much as a celebration of victory in war as a means to promote "international peace by arbitration and disarmament." To emphasize the international and peaceful character of the memorial, three British naval officers are buried here alongside three American naval officers—all of them killed during the Battle of Lake Erie.

BATTLE OF THE THAMES
Thamesville, Ontario

FOLLOWING THE CALAMITOUS DEFEAT of Commander Barclay's fleet, General Proctor could see no reasonable alternative but to abandon Forts Detroit and Malden and

A furious charge of mounted Kentucky riflemen smashes through General Proctor's lines near the River Thames in Ontario, scattering the British in all directions.

retreat eastward. Tecumseh, whose warriors provided a substantial portion of Proctor's fighting force, objected strenuously to the general's decision.

"Father, listen!" pleaded the great chief. "We are very much astonished to see our father tying up everything and preparing to run away. We wish to remain here and fight our enemy."

However, without the help of the British, Tecumseh had no means of feeding or otherwise supplying the warriors who followed him. Indeed hundreds if not thousands of his warriors despaired of the British cause—and perhaps their own as well—and slipped off into the wilderness. Having no real choice, Tecumseh and 500 still loyal braves joined in the retreat of Proctor's small army.

Encumbered by women and children and critically short of food, Proctor's column managed to cover only a few miles each day. General Harrison, who had disembarked on the banks of the Detroit River with several thousand men during the last week of September, was soon in hot pursuit. Harrison caught up with Proctor's fleeing forces on October 5 about 50 miles east of Detroit not far from the present-day town of Thamesville.

Proctor decided to make his stand on a stretch of swampy, wooded ground along the River Thames. The British general arranged his 800 regulars and militia in a long, thin line with Tecumseh's warriors in the forest on the right. Having made no effort to fortify their position, Proctor's men faced daunting odds as more than 3,000 American infantry and cavalry advanced on them from the west.

The battle had barely gotten underway when General Harrison ordered a large cavalry unit made up mostly of Kentucky riflemen to charge the center of the British line.

Caught by surprise, most of the British infantrymen barely had time to get off a shot, and their one small cannon failed to fire. The charge proved overwhelmingly successful as the Kentuckians rode right through the British, scattering them in all directions. The result was that Proctor fled the field accompanied by fewer than 250 of his men. The rest surrendered to the Americans.

With the British out of the way, Harrison was now able to turn his attention to the Indians, and his riders regrouped for a second charge. This time, however, they were stopped cold by determined musket fire. Tecumseh had decided that he would retreat no further and would make his last stand here. As the chief had earlier said to Proctor: "Our lives are in the hands of the Great Spirit. We are determined to defend our lands, and if it is his will, we wish to leave our bones upon them."

Although Harrison's riders were thrown back, Tecumseh was killed while exhorting his warriors to repel the Americans. With their leader dead, the Indians abandoned their position and retreated into the wilds. It may be that they carried Tecumseh's body with them since Harrison's men never located the corpse. Some of Tecumseh's most faithful followers said that he had been "carried up into the sky."

The casualties of the battle were comparatively small, with the American, British, and Indian forces each suffering only about thirty killed and wounded. Approximately 600 British

Tecumseh and his proud warriors refused to retreat with their British allies at the Thames River. The great Shawnee leader was killed in the fighting, and his dream of a tribal confederacy died with him.

soldiers surrendered. As it turned out, however, the scale of the British and Native American defeat proved far greater than the casualty list would suggest. Throughout the remainder of the war, the crown would not be able to field another effective army in the West. Along with Tecumseh, the dream of a tribal confederacy died. With it vanished the last realistic Native American opportunity to resist the advance of white civilization.

WHAT YOU'LL SEE TODAY

THE PLACE WHERE CHIEF TECUMSEH fell is now marked by a handsome stone monument and bronze plaque placed by the Historic Sites and Monuments Board of Canada. It is located beside a sweeping bend in the Thames River just off Highway 2 near Thamesville, Ontario. The area around the monument has not been heavily developed and provides a good sense of what this part of Canada may have looked like at the time Tecumseh made his last desperate stand. Incidentally, the name Tecumseh is well known hereabouts. The town of Chatham not far from Thamesville has a Tecumseh Public School as well as a city park, roadhouse, gas station, travel agency, and auto upholstery shop all named for the great chief.

British, Canadian, and Native American forces blunted the U.S. thrust across the Niagara at Queenston, but not before their heroic General Isaac Brock was fatally struck in the chest while attempting to retake the heights. Brock's beloved charger Alfred was also killed in the battle.

2

Niagara Theater
THUNDER BESIDE THE FALLS

ACCORDING TO AN OFTEN REPEATED LEGEND, a group of American officers from
Fort Niagara were having dinner with a group of British soldiers at Fort George in Canada
when word arrived that the United States had declared war on Great Britain.

It is said that both the dinner guests and their Canadian hosts received the news with
remarkable calm and grace. Everyone shook hands and wished one another well in the
approaching conflict. The Americans then walked down to the water, climbed into a boat,
and rowed back across the Niagara River toward a future that must have seemed to them
very uncertain. No doubt, their acquaintances in Canada were equally unsure of what the
coming days would bring.

Relations had been friendly along the border between the United States and the British
provinces of Upper and Lower Canada. Perhaps they were especially congenial here on the
Niagara, but they were not destined to remain so for long. A storm called the War of 1812
was about to break. Soon, former friends at Fort Niagara and Fort George, the strongly
defended British military post just on the other side of the river, would be exchanging
artillery fire almost daily. There would be bloody and destructive assaults back and forth

across the border, and there would be no social dinner engagements, such as the one mentioned above, for years to come.

In fact, the fighting would prove particularly desperate and brutal in this theater of the war. Geography had dictated this for there was no more strategically placed stretch of water in North America than the foaming torrent known as the Niagara. Only 35 miles (54 kilometers) long, the river and its legendary falls drained the overflow from Lakes Erie, Huron, Michigan, and Superior, a mighty expanse of water stretching deep into the continental interior. During the early nineteenth century, a combination of swamps, bogs, rugged hills, impenetrable forests, and a general lack of roads made it extremely difficult to reach the western frontier by way of any overland route. However, the Great Lakes and the rivers that flowed into or out of them made it much easier to move people and produce back and forth from western settlements. These waterways also made it relatively easy to transport troops, weapons, and military supplies to distant outposts. For all these reasons, political and military leaders on both warring sides recognized the vital importance of the Niagara River and the portage around Niagara Falls. Obviously, whoever controlled them would likely win the war in the West.

The peninsula squeezed between the waters of Lake Ontario to the north and Lake Erie to the south became one of the key battlegrounds of the war, with fighting surging back and forth across the rushing Niagara River.

America's Fort Niagara and the British stronghold at Fort George were located directly across from one another on opposite banks of the Niagara River.

Since the end of the Revolutionary War, the Niagara had served as both a natural and political boundary between U.S.- and British-held territory. The river's swift water and dangerous rapids made crossing from one side to the other a risky undertaking even in time of peace. Even so, both sides understood that the river *could* be crossed by a determined enemy, and so the Niagara Peninsula was seen as a sort of bridge across the lakes and into the vulnerable heartland of New York or Upper Canada.

Consequently, the Niagara border was strongly defended by a string of forts and military posts. On the British side, Fort Erie guarded the river entrance at the northeastern end of Lake Erie while a couple of days' march to the north Fort George kept watch over the mouth of the river near the southwestern end of Lake Ontario. On the American bank of the river, across from Fort George, U.S. troops garrisoned at Fort Niagara, the oldest and sturdiest of the Niagara fortifications. The fighting in the Niagara region was to prove so hot and vigorous that all three of these forts would fall to assaults by one side or the other. Fort George was captured, burned, recaptured, and rebuilt. Fort Erie would change hands four times in little more than two years of fighting. Fort Niagara fell to the British in a lightening night assault on December 18, 1813, and it remained in their hands for the rest of the war.

Officials in the United States saw the Niagara not just as a key link between the lakes but also as an inviting route for an invasion of Canada. Fort Niagara lay within easy striking distance of York (now Toronto), the capital of Upper Canada. A successful push into Canada at this point would sever Britain's eastern provinces from the west and leave British military forces in North America with few good options.

The Americans had hoped to win the war with three quick thrusts into Canada, one from the east toward the St. Lawrence River and Montreal, another from the west across the Detroit River, and a third over the Niagara and deep into Upper Canada. As it turned out, all three of these early invasion attempts ended in dismal failure. The attack across the Niagara was thrown back—almost literally—from Queenston Heights after having pushed less than a mile beyond the border.

Except for the constant roar of nearby Niagara Falls, Queenston was a quiet village before the War of 1812, but the thunder of cannon would be heard here often once the war began.

The Niagara Theater would feature many fierce engagements. Fighting flared at Thorold, Stoney Creek, Grimsby, Chippawa, Lundy's Lane, and elsewhere on or near the banks of the Niagara and to the west along the southern shores of Lake Ontario. Men and women on both sides would prove their mettle here, and their acts of great heroism—and sometimes barbarity—would not soon be forgotten.

QUEENSTON HEIGHTS BATTLEFIELD
Queenston, Ontario

DURING THE AUTUMN OF 1812, approximately 6,000 American troops gathered along the Niagara in preparation for an invasion of Canada. More than 3,500 of these were stationed at Lewiston across the river from a commanding eminence known as Queenston Heights. The latter force had been placed under the leadership of General Stephen Van Rensselaer, a politician with very little experience as a military commander. Unfortunately for Van Rensselaer, less than one-third of his soldiers were trained regulars. The rest were unruly militia unused to following orders and lacking a strong commitment to their nation's war aims—particularly the plan to conquer Canada.

The outnumbered British regulars, Canadian militia, and Indian warriors on the opposite shore were under the command of the brave and resourceful Isaac Brock. Only a few weeks earlier General Brock had outmaneuvered and defeated the largest American army on the northwestern frontier and seized Fort Detroit. Now he sought a way to prevent the Americans from crossing the Niagara. Believing the formidable U.S. forces across the river had been assembled for a strike on Fort George, Brock concentrated most of his forces there. To guard against a possible flanking attack upriver, he relied on a single company of grenadiers and a detachment of militia dug in on Queenston Heights.

General Isaac Brock was quick to respond to the October 13, 1812 American assault on the west bank of the Niagara.

Shown here crossing the swift Niagara, the Americans soon seized strategic Queenston Heights. However, they were eventually driven back and defeated by a mixed force of British regulars, Canadian militia, and Iroquois warriors.

Brock had expected an attack during the late summer or early fall, but by the second week of October it began to look as if the Americans might not be coming at all. Hampered by a lack of supplies and bedeviled by subordinate officers who often refused to obey his orders, Van Rensselaer delayed the U.S. offensive for several weeks. Finally, a few hours before dawn on October 13, he unleashed an amphibious assault on the tiny village of Queenston, situated at the foot of heights.

The first wave of the attack consisted of 300 volunteers crammed into thirteen small boats—the only useful watercraft the Americans could manage to assemble. These men, having struggled mightily to avoid being swept downstream by the strong Niagara current, scrambled onto Canadian soil, where they were quickly pinned down by the grenadiers on the heights. Because of the highly effective British and Canadian rifle and cannon fire, the Americans had great difficulty ferrying reinforcements across the swift Niagara.

With the approach of dawn, the British guns became even more accurate, and for a time, it appeared the invasion force would be driven back into the river. However, the hard-pressed U.S. troops clinging to the riverbank were about to execute a surprise maneuver that might have decisively changed the course of the battle if not of the war itself.

Captain John Wool, a 23-year-old American infantry officer, had located a path that wound around behind the British guns near the summit of the heights some 350 feet above the river. Although wounded during the landing, Wool led his men on a stealthy assent that reached the V-shaped redan containing the British cannon just after first light. Wool ordered an immediate assault that quickly overran the lightly defended British position.

Coincidentally, General Brock happened to be in the redan when the Americans attacked. Having been awakened by the distant rumble of cannon, Brock had mounted his faithful charger Alfred at Fort George and rushed to the scene of the fighting at full gallop. He had just climbed the heights to get a better view of the unfolding battle when Wool and his men appeared and opened fire. Brock and his artillerymen had just enough time to spike the cannon and escape down the slope toward Queenston.

Shocked by this development, Brock quickly organized a counterattack. He was far too good a soldier not to recognize the vital importance of the heights. They were, in fact, the key to the whole battle, and he knew it. When a first attempt to retake the heights was driven back by crackling American volleys, Brock ordered a second, and this time led the attack himself. An extraordinarily tall man, Brock made a target that was hard to miss, and before he had gotten halfway up the slope he was struck in the chest by a well-aimed shot from above. More likely than not, Brock died instantly, but according to legend, he offered some final words of encouragement to his men.

"Push on, brave volunteers!" Brock is said to have cried out before death overtook him.

Whether or not Brock actually said this, his men certainly made a brave effort to take back the British guns. Burning with desire for revenge, Brock's leaderless soldiers continued with their assault in the face of withering fire from the Americans. They had nearly succeeded in pushing their foes off the heights before they, too, were driven back.

With good reason, Van Rensselaer now began to believe that his men had won the first American victory of the war—and a smashing one at that. All that remained to ensure success was to secure the heights with reinforcements. With this in mind, the general ordered unit after unit to cross the Niagara and climb the heights. Some of his men stepped into the boats and obeyed, but most did not. The bloodcurdling cries of Indian warriors across the river and the site of boatloads of wounded coming back from the battlefield had greatly discouraged Van Rensselaer's lightly trained militiamen. Claiming that the terms of their militia service contracts did not require them to serve in a foreign country, they simply refused to go. The exasperated Van Rensselaer would later voice his frustration in his official report on the battle.

Placed in charge of U.S. troops along the Niagara frontier at the start of the war, General Stephen Van Rensselaer had little military experience.

"I urged the men to pass over the river, but in vain," said the general. "To my utter astonishment, I found that at the very moment when complete victory was in our hands, the ardor of the unengaged troops had entirely subsided."

Several hundred American soldiers were already on the Canadian side of the river, and with enemy fire increasing by the minute, evacuating them had become impossible. Unable to withdraw and without reinforcements, they were doomed. Standing alone on the heights, they could look down the hill and see the overwhelming British forces marshalling against them.

British General Roger Sheaffe had arrived from Fort George and taken over command from the mortally wounded Brock. Sheaffe brought reinforcements with him, and more were pouring in from Chippawa and other nearby British posts. By the middle of the afternoon, the Americans on the heights, now under the command of Colonel Winfield Scott, were significantly outnumbered, and soon they would be outmaneuvered as well. A bayonet attack by British regulars struck the Americans on one flank while a wave of whooping Iroquois hit them on the other. Caught in a vice of hot lead and cold steel, Scott's men were forced off the heights and down to the edge of the river where they were left with no choice but to surrender.

In all, nearly 1,000 Americans were trapped on the Canadian side of the Niagara and captured by the British. The militiamen were paroled and returned to the United States, while the regulars were sent to prison camps. American battlefield casualties amounted to approximately 200 either seriously wounded or killed. Only about half that many British troops and fewer than a dozen Iroquois fell in the process of defending or retaking the heights.

The relatively modest casualty figures for the Battle of Queenston Heights belie its considerable importance. A second American invasion attempt had been stopped almost as soon as it began, and this failure would have the effect of forestalling a third invasion, the planned advance on Montreal. While the British and Canadians exulted in their success at Queenston, they, too, had suffered a telling blow. The bullet that struck down Isaac Brock had robbed them of one of the most determined and capable commanders of the war.

However, the battle's true significance can better be understood by considering what might have happened if the Americans had won. Had they been able to hold the heights, they might have driven a wedge not just into the Niagara frontier but into Canada as a whole. Such a success likely would have rallied far greater support for the war especially among the reluctant northeastern militias while at the same time discouraging Britain's Indian allies. If all this had led to the conquest of a substantial portion of British/Canadian territory, the United States might very well have won the war before the end of 1812.

WHAT YOU'LL SEE TODAY

THERE IS MUCH TO SEE IN THE VICINITY of Queenston Heights, now one of Canada's many well-tended National Historic Sites. Located off the scenic Niagara Parkway and just across the Niagara River from the United States, the site offers an interpretive trail with plaques that highlight several key stages of the battle: the initial *Attack* (Marker 1), Wool's climb up the *Treacherous River Cliff* (Marker 2), the *Capture of the Redan* and the *Death of Brock* (Marker 3), the *Counteroffensive* organized by Seaffe (Marker 4), and the *Decisive Battle* consisting of flank attacks on the American position (Marker 5). Also on the heights are the ruins of Fort Drummond and Fort Riall, a pair of British strong points constructed later in the war.

In the nearby village of Queenston is the Brock Monument, a 185-foot (56-meter) stone cylinder erected here during the late nineteenth century to commemorate General Brock's service to the crown and to Canada. Originally, the general's remains were buried here, but they are now interred in the Queenston village cemetery. Not far from the Brock monument is a much smaller memorial dedicated to Alfred, Brock's beloved charger who, like his master, was killed in the fighting.

Likewise in Queenston is the historic Laura Secord House located at the corner of Partition and Queenston Streets. A heroine known well to Canadian school children, Laura Secord helped save the life of her wounded husband James who served the British cause at Queenston Heights as a sergeant of the militia. The following year, a piece of information acquired by Mrs. Secord would play a pivotal role in the Battle of Beaver Dams. Damaged during the fighting at Queenston, the Secord House has been handsomely restored and serves as a museum.

FORT GEORGE
Niagara-on-the-Lake, Ontario

HAVING BEEN FORCED TO HAND Fort Niagara over to the Americans by the Jay Treaty concluded in 1796, the British lost what had long been considered the most significant military post on the Great Lakes. To maintain a strong presence in the Niagara region, the British established Fort George at the mouth of the river just across from their former stronghold. The fort consisted of half a dozen earthen bastions and a number of barracks and other buildings protected by a heavy timber stockade.

After war broke out during the summer of 1812, artillerymen here frequently exchanged cannon fire with their counterparts at Fort Niagara across the river. Lobbed toward their targets from a considerable distance, these artillery rounds had little telling effect, and for nearly a year no one attempted a direct attack on either fortress. Then, on May 27, 1813, the Americans launched a large-scale amphibious assault using their Lake Ontario fleet to land troops behind Fort George. Supported by more than a dozen ships, the U.S. assault force of nearly 5,000 infantry soon forced the outnumbered British to abandon the fort and retreat. Nearly half of the 1,400-man garrison was killed, wounded, or captured. The rest fled toward Burlington about 30 miles (50 kilometers) to the west.

The Americans then hurriedly repaired Fort George and made it their head-quarters for another attempted inva-sion of Canada. However, their push westward toward Burlington was soon blunted at the Battle of Stoney Creek. Later, after an abortive raid ended in an ignominious defeat at the Battle of Beaver Dams, U.S. forces withdrew

Fort George was one of the most important British military posts in the Great Lakes region.

behind a defensive perimeter anchored by the fort. By December, they had withdrawn across the river, but not before burning what remained of Fort George and the nearby town of Newark. Angry British and Canadian troops would later seek revenge for the destruction of the town. Once the British reclaimed Fort George, they held it for the remainder of the war.

WHAT YOU'LL SEE TODAY

FORT GEORGE, A NATIONAL HISTORIC SITE maintained by Parks Canada, offers an insightful glimpse of British military life during the early nineteenth century. Once within its walls of earth and wood, visitors may think they have been transported 200 years into the past. Modern-day interpreters often wear period dress to enhance the illusion, and occa-sionally, a fife can be heard playing marshal music. Tours of the bastions, barracks, and mess halls reveal them to be sturdy but far from snug. Obviously, the soldiers stationed here were prepared to sacrifice comfort in exchange for a better chance of survival when under attack.

Fort George is immediately adjacent the historic town of Niagara-on-the-Lake, once known as Newark. Having long ago risen from the ashes of its wartime destruction, it is now a popular tourist destination alive with art galleries, elegant boutiques, ice cream shops, wineries, and fancy restaurants. Also of interest is nearby Fort Mississauga, a star-shaped fort built by the British in 1814 to bolster the defensive capabilities of the adjacent, thoroughly battered Fort George. The fort consists of earthen battlements reinforced by a massive brick blockhouse.

The War of 1812

STONEY CREEK BATTLEFIELD

Hamilton, Ontario

AFTER THE AMERICANS CAPTURED Fort George during the late spring of 1813, the doorway to Canada appeared to be standing ajar. Hard-pressed British forces along the Niagara fell back toward the western end of Lake Ontario, and General Henry Dearborn's victorious infantry followed hoping to force a confrontation. If they could sweep aside the remaining British resistance, the way would be open to invade Upper Canada and drive a wedge into Britain's remaining North American colonies. To prevent this, approximately 1,600 British regulars under General John Vincent dug in on Burlington Heights, an expanse of elevated ground overlooking the lake.

About a week after the fall of Fort George, the British on the heights acquired some unwelcome neighbors. By June 5, the American advance had reached Stoney Creek, a gurgling water course a few miles short of Vincent's defenses. That night a detachment of 1,300 U.S. troops serving under Generals William Winder and John Chandler, a Dearborn subordinate,

Fought in the middle of the night, the Battle of Stoney Creek was a confused affair with soldiers on both sides unsure of their targets.

bedded down along its banks. Unfortunately for the Americans, who likely felt the British were beaten and on the run, they did not bother to fortify their camp. Nor did they manage to adequately safeguard the password that allowed sentries to tell friend from foe. Somehow the password, which was "Wil-Hen-Har," an abbreviation of William Henry Harrison, fell into the hands of Vincent's adjutant, Colonel John Harvey. With this vital piece of intelligence in hand, Harvey resolved to hit the Americans hard while they slept.

Along with 700 hand-picked men, Harvey crept toward the U.S. camp and arrived there shortly after midnight. The password enabled them to silence the American sentries before they could raise an alarm, and with bayonets fixed, the British rushed the camp. Although considerably outnumbered, Harvey's men managed to throw their surprised enemies into complete confusion. A wild melee ensued with musket and canon flashes lighting up the night. By dawn, both sides had withdrawn, but the badly shaken Americans eventually retreated all the way back to Fort George. They left behind more than 50 of their men either killed or wounded. About 100 of the Americans were taken prisoner, including their commanders, General Winder and General Chandler.

The engagement had been so chaotic that the British thought their own commander, General Vincent, had been captured by the Americans. Instead, he had gotten so thoroughly lost in the dark that it took him more than 24 hours to find his way back to his headquarters. Overall the battle had been costly for the British, whose casualties exceeded 150. Nonetheless, Vincent was pleased with the results of the engagement as it had halted the American advance and secured the upper Niagara Peninsula from invasion. The Americans never attempted another attack on Burlington Heights.

WHAT YOU'LL SEE TODAY

ACCESSIBLE FROM KING STREET and Centennial Parkway in the community of Stoney Creek, now part of Hamilton, Ontario, Battlefield Park preserves the site of this important clash of arms. The 15-acre park includes the late-eighteenth-century Gage House, which served as the American headquarters during battle. Known today as the Battlefield House, the lovely old two-story building contains a small but highly informative museum. Nearby, the 100-foot-tall Stoney Creek Battlefield Monument stands on the site of the American encampment along the creek. The monument consists of a slender gray stone tower rising from the middle of a castellated stone blockhouse. Also in Stoney Creek is the impressive Stone Lion Monument, which marks the burial place of British, Canadian, and American soldiers who died here. The monument features a mosaic Union Jack and a statue of a growling lion.

BEAVER DAMS BATTLEFIELD
Thorold, Ontario

FOR SEVERAL WEEKS FOLLOWING their retreat from Stoney Creek, American forces remained holed up at Fort George. During this time, their pickets were constantly harassed by a small forward British detachment under Lieutenant James Fitzgibbon. By the third week of June 1813, the Americans had enough of Fitzgibbon and launched a punitive expedition aimed at killing or capturing the scrappy British officer and driving off his troops. On June 23, a considerable force of 500 U.S. infantry supported by two field cannon set off in the direction of Fitzgibbon's headquarters, a stone house located in what is today the town of Thorold, Ontario. During their first night on the march, the Americans camped in and around the village

Completed many years after the event, the evocative painting on the right depicts Laura Secord warning Lieutenant James Fitzgibbon that U.S. troops were approaching his position west of the Niagara. Armed with this vital information, Fitzgibbon ambushed and defeated the Americans at Beaver Dams. The postage stamp on the left honors the Canadian heroine.

of Queenston on the west bank of the Niagara. At this point the energetic patriotism of a young Canadian settler named Laura Secord intervened in the course of events. A year earlier, Secord had been driven from her home by the fighting around Queenston. She had spent the time since nursing back to health her husband James who was wounded at the Battle of Queenston Heights. Now, more than eight months after that pivotal battle, American troops were once more in Queenston, and as it turned out, Laura Secord happened to overhear their officers discussing the planned attack on Fitzgibbon's command.

She then set out cross country to warn her countrymen. Secord walked at least 12 miles through rough, wooded terrain before stumbling into the camp of Native American warriors allied to the British. The Indians then led her to Fitzgibbon's outpost where she delivered her vital information.

Armed with this intelligence, Fitzgibbon prepared a nasty surprise for the advancing Americans. Early on the morning of June 24 in a stretch of dense timber just east of the settlement of Beaver Dams, they were attacked on both flanks by 50 British regulars and as many as 400 Iroquois Indians. The U.S. troops under Colonel Charles Boerstler fought back briefly but soon surrendered.

The battle proved a disastrous psychological blow for the Americans, convincing them that they could not safely maneuver in country held by the British and their Indian allies. Not only had the Battle of Beaver Dams cost them hundreds of men and a large quantity of valuable supplies, it sharply limited their offensive options west of the Niagara. Afterward, the Americans were effectively bottled up at Fort George and by the end of the year had abandoned the fort itself.

WHAT YOU'LL SEE TODAY

A SIMPLE STONE MONUMENT IN Thorold's Battle of Beaver Dams Park commemorates the British and Native American victory. However, the cairn-style monument does not mark the actual site of the battle, most of which was destroyed during construction of the Welland Canal. The Decew House where Fitzgibbon met with Laura Secord burned in 1950, but the ruins located off Decew Road are still visible.

Among the most historic sites in North America, Fort Niagara dates to the early eighteenth century, when the French reinforced a rustic frontier outpost on Lake Ontario at the mouth of the Niagara River.

FORT NIAGARA
Youngstown, New York

ESTABLISHED BY THE FRENCH DURING the late seventeenth century on what was then a wild frontier, Fort Niagara would dominate the mouth of the Niagara River for more than a century. In 1726, the French reinforced the remote outpost with the massive two-story structure they described to local Indians as a "House of Peace," but which is better known today as the "French Castle." Later on they added hefty stone walls with ramparts and revetments—converting what was essentially a trading post into the strongest fortress west of the Alleghenies. During the French and Indian War, the fort fell to British forces after a 19-day siege. The British considered Fort Niagara so important that they held onto it until long after the Revolutionary War even though it was technically located on U.S. soil. The fort was finally ceded to the Americans under terms of the Jay Treaty in 1796.

During early stages of the War of 1812, Fort Niagara served as a base for U.S. operations against Queenston Heights, Fort George, and other British positions west of the Niagara River. When the Americans' 1813 campaign in the western Niagara region collapsed, the British resolved to retaliate with a series of punishing strikes east of the river. They aimed their first blow at Fort Niagara itself.

On the night of December 18, 1813, a detachment of 550 British infantrymen quietly crossed the river using boats that had been secretly dragged overland to the banks of the Niagara. Under the command of Colonel John Murray, the British landed south of the fort and crept through the dark toward its outer defenses. Thinly garrisoned and in poor repair, Fort Niagara was ill prepared to resist a siege, but as things turned out, none would be necessary. A small party of negligent American pickets were surprised while playing cards at a local tavern and forced at bayonet point to reveal the fort's password. With this, the advance members of the assault force, the so-called "forlorn hope," managed to cross the fort's drawbridge unmolested.

Using bayonets rather than bullets, the British then began to slaughter the sleeping men within the walls. The battle was over quickly, with most of the garrison surrendering. However, some of the defenders barricaded themselves in Fort Niagara's massive South Redoubt. When they refused to lay down their arms, Murray ordered his men to rush the building and offer no quarter to those inside. As many as eighty Americans were bayoneted during the fighting and more than 300 others were taken prisoner. British casualties amounted to only eleven killed and wounded. In addition to the fort's garrison and its senior officer, Captain Nathaniel Leonard, the British captured a significant quantity of military equipment and supplies.

General John Drummond, overall commander of British forces in the Niagara region, had conceived of the attack on Fort Niagara, and he was anxious to avenge the burning of Newark during the recent American invasion. With Fort Niagara in hand, he ordered a series of destructive raids on U.S. towns and villages, including Lewiston and Buffalo. The British would retain control of Fort Niagara until the end of the war, and it would help protect the northern flank of their army during the American's 1814 campaign west of the Niagara.

Re-enactors on a fortress parade ground relive the War of 1812.

WHAT YOU'LL SEE TODAY

LOCATED OFF THE NORTH END of New York's scenic Robert Moses Parkway, Old Fort Niagara immerses visitors in its own extraordinary history. The flags of three nations have flown over the fort, and appropriately enough, the royal fleur-de-lis of the French and the British Union Jack still flap above its battlements alongside Old Glory. The fort is open year-round. In the summer, guides dressed in military uniforms typical of the 1812 era conduct tours. The daily musket demonstrations are especially popular with children. Of particular interest is the two-story stone French Castle, one of the oldest buildings on the Great Lakes if not in all of North America.

What was then the village of Buffalo was burned by British troops during General Drummond's winter offensive in December and January of 1813-1814. Drummond undertook the offensive and the devastation of Buffalo, Black Rock, and Lewiston in part for strategic reasons but also in retaliation for destructive American attacks on York, Newark, and other Canadian villages. Little remains to recall the burning of Buffalo other than a few scattered signs and plaques. One of these, a Seaway Trail marker in Naval and Serviceman's Park, describes the burning. Also in Buffalo is a statue of Commodore Oliver Hazard Perry standing not far from the shores of Lake Erie in the city's waterside Front Park.

CHIPPAWA BATTLEFIELD
Niagara Parkway, Ontario

WITH THE DEFEAT OF NAPOLEON appearing imminent in 1814, American leaders were anxious to make one last attempt to invade Canada before large numbers of British troops could be transferred to North America. Once again the Niagara region figured prominently in their plans. In early July an invasion force of several thousand men under General Jacob Brown crossed the Niagara, captured Fort Erie, and then marched northward along the left bank of the river.

On the morning of July 5, General Phineas Riall and a detachment of approximately 2,100 seasoned British troops attempted to block Brown's advance. Believing that he was still facing only a small part of the invading army, Riall concluded that an immediate attack was

During the 1814 summer campaign west of the Niagara, the deft maneuvers of surprisingly well-trained U.S. Army regulars shocked the British, who had expected to face undisciplined militia. American infantry and artillerymen fought with determination at Chippawa, Lundy's Lane, and Fort Erie.

his best option. Hoping to catch his opponents off guard, he sent his men pouring across Chippawa Creek into the flat fields just north of the American positions. The British moved forward in straight lines with the river on their left, a dense forest on their right, and the creek at their backs.

Often in the past British regulars had been able to cow the Americans with their gleaming bayonets and disciplined maneuvers, but not this time. Having benefited from many weeks of training under the direction of the capable Winfield Scott, Brown's men quickly formed orderly battle lines and engaged the British with musket and cannon. The Americans soon got the better of the artillery duel, and their musket fire also proved more accurate and deadly. The turning point of battle came when the left and right wings of the American line angled inward so that they could fire on the British flanks.

Riall had thought that most of the U.S. infantry on the field that day would be composed of undisciplined militia. However, upon witnessing the breathtaking precision of the American maneuvers he is said to have exclaimed: "Those are regulars, by God!" Seeing that his own redcoat regulars were taking a severe pounding, Riall ordered them to retreat back across the Chippawa Bridge.

British casualties amounted to 400 killed and wounded with 90 taken prisoner. The Americans lost about 300 men with none taken prisoner. In the days following the Battle of Chippawa, Brown continued to outmaneuver Riall, forcing him to retreat all the way to Fort George. Brown had failed to corner and decisively defeat the British. Even so, the excellent performance of his troops at Chippawa had shown for the first time that American forces could successfully engage British regulars in the open field.

WHAT YOU'LL SEE TODAY

LOCATED OFF THE NIAGARA PARKWAY a few miles north of Fort Erie, the Chippawa Battlefield is a must-see destination for anyone interested in the War of 1812 or in early-nineteenth-century military tactics. Unlike so many other historic sites, this one remains in near pristine condition. It appears little changed from that day two centuries ago when destiny brought the determined armies of Brown and Riall together in these fields. There are no gift shops here or guides in antique military attire and not much to see except for a modest memorial obelisk and the battlefield itself, but therein lies the magic of the place. Without all the well-meaning interpretive clutter, it is possible to gaze out over the woods and meadows and imagine the smoke and din of battle. A self-guided walking tour with simple but informative descriptive markers provides a good sense of the give and take of the action.

Just north of the battlefield, a plaque in King's Bridge Park marks the site of Fort Chippawa. General Riall and his troops briefly took refuge here after losing the Battle of Chippawa. The park is located only five minutes from Niagara Falls, and the thunder of that mighty cataract is plainly audible.

LUNDY'S LANE BATTLEFIELD
Niagara Falls, Ontario

UNFORTUNATELY FOR THE AMERICANS, General Brown could not follow up his victory at Chippawa with an attack on Fort George. Focused exclusively on defeating the British fleet, Commodore Isaac Chauncey steadfastly refused to bring the American Lake

The aggressive spirit shown by U.S. troops at Chippawa was in evidence again three weeks later at Lundy's Lane where the fighting went on until long after midnight. When the battle ended, however, it was the Americans who retreated.

This dramatic painting depicts the pivotal Battle of Lundy's Lane, which was fought mostly at night. Although it was one of the bloodiest confrontations of the war, the battle ended in a draw.

Ontario flotilla to Brown's assistance. This left Brown without the reinforcements, supplies, and siege artillery he needed to reduce the fort's defenses. Brown led a cautious advance northward along the Niagara, but having plundered and burned a few Canadian villages, his army fell back beyond Niagara Falls to the vicinity of Chippawa Creek. General Riall followed with about 1,000 regulars and militia pulled from behind the walls of Fort George and nearby Fort Mississauga. These troops he deployed along Lundy's Lane, a country road named for William Lundy, a local loyalist Quaker.

On July 25 Brown decided to move against the British position and ordered Winfield Scott to march northward on Queenston Road with a detachment of slightly more than 1,000 men. It was nearing 6 p.m. by the time this force came within sight of the British. Despite the coming of nightfall, the combative general deployed his soldiers into a line of battle and ordered them to attack.

The American assault was ferocious, particularly on the British left, which soon started to give ground. Believing he was outnumbered, Riall began to organize a retreat. Just at that moment, however, General Gordon Drummond arrived with reinforcements and ordered his subordinate to stand fast. General Brown soon reached the battlefield with reinforcements of his own, and as darkness fell over Lundy's Lane the struggle grew in both intensity and the number of men engaged.

Unused to fighting in the dark, troops on both sides had difficulty distinguishing their own positions from those of their enemies. The confusion was so great that soldiers sometimes trained musket and cannon fire upon their own men. Wounded in his left arm, General Riall became lost in the gloom and was captured by an American unit that had worked its way around the British left. Riall was the highest-ranking British military officer captured by the Americans during the war.

The battle went on far into the night with only the flash of igniting black powder and the bright trails of Congreve rockets to illuminate the scene. By 10 p.m. the focus of the battle had become a battery of British cannon arrayed in a hillside cemetery on the grounds of a small church house. Colonel James Miller and 300 American infantrymen had fought their way up the slope and captured the guns. Recognizing that this was likely the turning point of the battle, Drummond ordered an immediate counterattack aimed at recovering the guns. Three times the British charged up the hill, and three times they were driven back.

By midnight, the Americans seemed on the point of winning the battle. But at around that time the fortunes—or misfortunes—of war turned against them. General Brown and Scott, likely his most competent and aggressive subordinate, were both severely wounded in separate incidents. Brown had been struck in the thigh by a musket ball, and as his aides carried him from the field, he ordered his exhausted troops to retreat back toward Chippawa. Perhaps Brown believed his troops were too battered and tired to continue the battle or that there was no one left standing on the field he could trust to lead them on to victory. In any case, Brown's junior officers complied—though some objected strenuously—and pulled their

Instead of fireworks, these War of 1812 enthusiasts use cannon and musket fire to celebrate the historic Battle of Lundy's Lane.

men back. Among the last to withdraw were the bloodied American infantrymen who had so doggedly clung to the British hilltop battery. As it turned out, there were not enough horses available to remove the captured British cannon.

Brown's army fell back to Chippawa and, in the days that followed, retreated all the way to Fort Erie. The British, who had suffered no less than the Americans, did not immediately pursue. Casualties on each side amounted to more than 850 killed, wounded, and captured, making a statistical draw of what was certainly one of the most punishing battles ever fought in Canada.

WHAT YOU'LL SEE TODAY

THE BURGEONING CITY OF Niagara Falls, Ontario, has spread around and over much of the Lundy's Lane Battlefield. Lundy's Lane itself is now a busy city street lined with shops, restaurants, and strip malls. However, there is still a church on what is today known as Drummond Hill, and the ground over which much of the fighting happened remains a cemetery. A monument featuring General Drummond mounted on his charger marks the

In part because the battle was fought at night, there was much confusion at Lundy's Lane. Entire units got lost in the dark while wounded British General Phineas Riall fell prisoner to a detached company of American infantry.

cemetery's highest elevation where Drummond's battery once stood. A series of nearby plaques describe the bloody tug-of-war over the guns. Elsewhere in the cemetery are other markers and monuments related to the battle. The cemetery also features a monument dedicated to the War of 1812 Canadian heroine Laura Secord, who is buried here.

Incorporated Militia on the Niagara

During the winter of 1814, General Gordon Drummond assembled a battalion of militia by drawing together individual companies that had been raised in Kingston, Prescott, Cornwall, and other towns in Upper Canada. Referred to as the Incorporated Militia, this battalion of Canadian volunteers drilled at Fort George and soon became a cohesive and effective fighting unit. The Incorporated Militia was destined to play a pivotal role at the key Battle of Lundy's Lane. When the Americans threatened to turn the British and Canadian left flank, the Incorporated Militia turned to face the attack with parade-ground precision. Although suffering heavy losses, the Canadians managed to stem the American tide and hold their ground.

FORT ERIE
Fort Erie, Ontario

Established by the British in 1764, Fort Erie guarded the Niagara River entrance and the southern end of the Niagara Portage. Positioned just across Lake Erie from Buffalo, New York, this strategic earth-and-stone fortification changed hands several times during the war. At the beginning of the U.S. offensive in the late spring of 1813, the British garrison destroyed much of the fort before retreating to Burlington where they joined survivors from the Battle of Fort George. Six months later Fort Erie was reoccupied by the British during their winter counteroffensive.

Repairs to the walls and other defensive structures had still not been completed by July 3, 1814, when a large U.S. invasion force crossed the Niagara. The Fort Erie garrison of just 137 men under Major Thomas Buck could not hold out for long and was forced to surrender. Afterward, the Americans used the fort as a base for their northward advance along the west bank of the river. Following the bloody Battle of Lundy's Lane, the Americans fell back to Fort Erie and readied it for an expected British attack. It was not long in coming.

About a week after the battle, General Gordon Drummond arrived with 3,000 British troops and ordered them to establish siege lines. Drummond believed the Fort Erie garrison was relatively weak and would quickly surrender. Unknown to him, however, the Americans had stationed more than 2,000 men here, and they were led by General Edmund Gaines, a skilled and determined commander. Gaines and his men had extended and strengthened the walls of the fort and added several key gun emplacements.

For the next ten days, Drummond attempted unsuccessfully to reduce the fort's defenses with cannon fire. His cannon were not powerful enough to do significant damage, and cannonballs were literally bouncing off the walls. Finally, having concluded that Fort Erie would have to be taken by storm, Drummond devised a complex three-pronged assault on its well-defended walls. Two wings of the attack were supposed to strike the fort's outer defenses simultaneously from the north and south, while a third column closed in on the fort's main star-shaped bastion.

The officers responsible for executing Drummond's plan had little confidence in it. One even wrote a farewell note to his wife before commencing the operation. Almost as soon as the attack began in the early morning darkness of August 15, it became obvious that their qualms and disquiet had been warranted. A war party of Indians was supposed to have launched a noisy attack to distract the Americans, but the warriors arrived late and their whoops could barely be heard above the din of the battle. Neither of the flanking columns managed to reach their objectives before the crucial element of surprise was lost, and soon the unprotected British were being cut down in their hundreds by withering musket and cannon fire. Both assaults were repulsed with heavy losses, and Colonel Hercules Scott, who led the northern column, was struck in the head and killed by a musket ball.

The center prong of the attack proved more successful than the flanking columns had been and managed to fight its way into the bastion. Soon afterward, however, an ammunition storage magazine within the bastion ignited in a tremendous explosion that blew many of the attackers to bits. At this point the assault ended with the shattered British detachments hurrying back to their own lines. General Drummond's army had absorbed fearsome losses in the misfired attempt to take the fort, including more than 900 men killed, wounded, or captured. Total American casualties amounted to fewer than 100.

A month later the Americans, now under the command of the aggressive General Jacob Brown, countered with an attack of their own. In the midst of a torrential downpour on September 17 they struck three British batteries and managed to capture two of them and spike their guns before retreating. After this, General Drummond despaired of taking Fort Erie and retreated northward with his men to Chippawa. The Americans briefly considered a pursuit, but lacking badly needed reinforcements and supplies rejected the idea. By early autumn they had destroyed and abandoned the fort they had so tenaciously defended.

WHAT YOU'LL SEE TODAY

Meticulously restored during the 1930s, Fort Erie stands on the shores of Lake Erie near the south end of Ontario's Niagara Parkway. The restoration emphasizes many of the features typical of fortifications built during the eighteenth and early nineteenth centuries. The three-foot-thick stone curtain wall is surrounded by a deep moat-like ditch and reinforced by a broad earthen bank, or ravelin, designed to absorb cannon shot. Interpreters in period uniforms recount the history of the fort while restored barracks hint at what life was like for soldiers stationed at the fort. Outside the star-shaped bastion walls, a columnar stone monument marks the mass grave of more than 150 men killed during the 1814 siege.

Canada's Bloodiest Battle

More than 3,000 men fell during the late summer siege of Fort Erie in 1814, making this the costliest battle ever fought on Canadian soil. Nearly 2,000 were killed and wounded on August 15 alone during an all-out British assault of the walls of the fort. Soldiers who survived carried grisly memories of this bloody engagement with them to the grave. Jarvis Hanks, a British drummer boy, witnessed the explosion of a fortress bastion that killed hundreds of his comrades. Later he reported having seen a great pile of "legs, arms, and heads separated by the concussion from the trunks to which they had long been attached."

The war in the Lake Ontario Theater became a naval arms race, with each side building bigger and bigger ships in an all-out effort to outgun the other.

3
Lake Ontario Theater
WARSHIPS ON AN INLAND SEA

POSITIONED TO THE EAST OF NIAGARA FALLS, Lake Ontario is different from the other Great Lakes in that it has direct access to the Atlantic by way of the St. Lawrence River. However, this link to the ocean is sharply limited by narrows and stretches of swift, choppy water that make the upper reaches of the river extremely difficult, if not impossible to navigate. During the eighteenth and nineteenth centuries, large, ocean-going warships could not safely travel beyond Montreal, and only small trading vessels and canoes could make use of the entire length of the river. In the War of 1812 this meant that the fighting ships so vital to control of Lake Ontario and the region surrounding it had to be built on the shores of the lake itself. Consequently, the War of 1812 as it was fought in this theater evolved into an all-out naval arms race.

The British started the war on Lake Ontario with several fighting ships including the 22-gun mini-frigate *Royal George,* the 14-gun brig *Earl of Moira,* and the recently launched eight-gun schooner *Prince Regent.* These vessels were not part of the Royal Navy. Instead, they were manned and operated under the authority of the Provincial Marine, an arm of the British Army's quartermaster service. Although by no means impressive, the tiny Provincial Marine

The public in America, Canada, and Britain recognized the importance of naval power on the lakes. Shipbuilding even became the subject of political cartoons. This one shows a fictional John Bull baking a new fleet of British warships in a special oven.

fleet was more than a match for the U.S. Navy's lone Great Lakes warship, the 18-gun brig *Onieda* that had been launched in 1809.

Political and military leaders on both sides of the conflict understood only too well that the existing disparity in naval power on the lake was unlikely to remain fixed. Indeed, the three-to-one advantage in ships and guns the British held at the beginning of the war would not last long. Rushed to the shores of Lake Ontario with orders to reverse the imbalance, Commodore Isaac Chauncey purchased or commandeered every trading schooner he could find, outfitting them with whatever guns were available. Meanwhile, the keels of new fighting ships were laid at Sackets Harbor, New York, at the far eastern end of the lake. The Provincial Marine quickly responded with a construction program of its own. Thus, by the autumn of 1812, Sackets Harbor and the British/Canadian port of Kingston near the St. Lawrence River entrance had become the focus of frenetic, even desperate shipbuilding activity. In this way they played the same role in the war on Lake Ontario that Amherstburg and Presque Isle did in the struggle for control of Lake Erie. Because of their vital importance, the shipyards and other naval facilities at Kingston and Sackets Harbor were both attacked during the course of the war, but neither was ever decisively put out of action.

As was the case on Lake Erie, the tides of the conflict ebbed and flowed for one side or the other depending on their success in building superior fighting ships. While the edge in naval firepower had shifted to the Americans before the end of 1812, it had returned to the Provincial Marine by the spring of 1813. Later that same year, Chauncey's fleet once more gained the upper hand. The race for naval superiority would seesaw back and forth in this manner right up until the end of the war.

Surprisingly, the *potential* advantages held at one time or another by either the British or the Americans never translated into decisive action. Both Chauncey and his British counterpart, Captain James Yeo, understood only too well that the course of the war might be permanently altered by a single fleet engagement. In fact, Commodore Perry's victory on Lake Erie did turn the war in the Northwest decisively in favor of the Americans. However, with its central location between relatively populous regions of the United States and Upper Canada, Lake Ontario had far more strategic importance. A major naval victory—or defeat— here might determine the outcome of the entire war. Faced with such an all-or-nothing prospect, neither commander could bring himself to risk his fleet on the open waters of the lake. Instead, they continuously maneuvered their flotillas around one another and scurried for the safety of well-fortified ports whenever they felt threatened.

The unwillingness of Chauncey and Yeo to commit their fleets inevitably resulted in a stalemate, one with consequences extending far beyond the shores of Lake Ontario. Yeo might have brought an end to the war much earlier had he cornered and defeated Chauncey when he had the strength to do so. On the other hand, Chauncey's unwavering focus on the struggle for naval superiority prevented him from lending desperately needed support to U.S. ground forces. For example, after the Battle of Chippawa in July 1814, when General Jacob Brown appeared on the verge of driving the British out of the Niagara Peninsula, Chauncey refused to offer any meaningful assistance.

"For God's sake let me see you," Brown pleaded in a note written to Chauncey on July 13. "This army can march and fight all over the area if the fleet will carry the supplies."

Chauncey's reply was quite terse. He informed Brown in no uncertain terms that the American fleet on Lake Ontario had been ordered "to seek and fight the enemy fleet" and that it would not be diverted "by any sinister attempt to render us subordinate to, or an appendage of, the Army."

Without the help of Chauncey's fleet, Brown was soon forced to give up on what had begun as a very promising campaign. Meanwhile, Chauncey and Yeo kept building, to no particular purpose, ever larger and more powerful ships. As the war entered its final stages during the fall of 1814, the British launched the *St. Lawrence* at Kingston. A 112-gun behemoth larger than a typical British seagoing ship-of-the-line, the *St. Lawrence* never saw combat. Nor did Chauncey and Yeo ever meet in all-out battle on the lake.

When they ventured onto the open waters of Lake Ontario, British and American commanders were wary of any confrontation with the enemy. Neither side dared commit themselves to a battle that might destroy their fleets and lose the war.

FORT FREDERICK
Kingston, Ontario

LIKE FORT MACKINAC, FORT MALDEN, Fort Niagara, and several of the other key British or American strong points scattered throughout the Great Lakes region, Fort Frederick guarded an intersection of waterways. Not far from the fort and the adjacent settlement of Kingston, the abundant waters of Lake Ontario flowed into the St. Lawrence River beginning the final 600-mile leg of their journey eastward to the Atlantic. Established during the late 1700s, the fort was destined to become one of the most important British bases along the entire length of the border between the United States and Canada. However, its importance stemmed not so much in its geographic location as from the naval base that stood on the banks of nearby Navy Bay.

The Kingston naval dockyard built and maintained supply vessels and fighting ships for the Provincial Marine. The six-gun schooner *Duke of Gloucester* was built here in 1807 at about the time the *Chesapeake* incident started the United States and Great Britain down the road toward war. Two years later, the Kingston yards launched the 21-gun sloop *Royal George,* which helped give the Provincial Marine an edge on Lake Ontario during the early months of the war.

The British advantage in guns and ships had all but evaporated by the fall of 1812 when Commodore Isaac Chauncey set out from Sackets Harbor with a fleet capable of challenging the British. Commanding a flotilla of seven vessels including the *Oneida* and an assortment of smaller fighting ships, Chauncey attempted to seize control of the lake. On November 8, he caught up with the *Royal George* a few miles west of Kingston, and the *Oneida*, along with the armed schooners *Conquest, Julia, Pert,* and *Growler* opened up on the British ship with their long guns. Outnumbered and outgunned, the *Royal George* fled into Kingston Harbor, but the American fleet followed and continued to pepper her with iron. Eventually, the brisk cannonade forced the *Royal George* to take refuge beside the Kingston wharves where ground troops could help keep the Americans at a distance. Also rendering assistance were the cannons of Fort Frederick located at the tip of Point Frederick across the bay.

As darkness approached, Chauncey ordered his ships to stand off and drop anchor in open water just outside the harbor. He intended to renew his attack on the *Royal George* in the morning if the winds proved favorable. They did not, so Chauncey took his fleet back to Sackets Harbor believing that he and his men had already won a significant victory at Kingston. In fact, the American attack had done little damage to either the *Royal George* or to the naval facilities at Kingston. Even so, it had demonstrated American naval strength on Lake Ontario and left Chauncey in control of its strategic waters for the remainder of the year. Alarmed by these developments, the British responded by bolstering their

Fighting Ships on the Lakes

Most of the warships that served on the Great Lakes during the War of 1812 were small schooners, sloops, brigs, or gunboats. Many were converted merchant ships while others were specially built for either the U.S. Navy or Provincial Marine at shipyards in Kingston, Sackets Harbor, York, Presque Isle, or Amherstburg. Typically, these modest vessels displaced no more than a few hundred tons and rarely carried more than 20 guns. Larger, more heavily armed ships were constructed only during the latter stages of the war on Lake Ontario where the two sides labored feverishly to outbuild and outgun one another.

Rigged fore-and-aft much like a modern sailboat, these Great Lakes fighting ships were relatively nimble and able to sail into the wind. However, because they were hurriedly built or were never intended for warfare in the first place, they tended to be fragile and difficult to handle, especially in windy conditions. Overloaded with guns, they were often top-heavy and prone to capsize in storms—a tendency made worse by the inherent choppiness of fresh water. Ironically, the British and American lake fleets lost far more vessels and sailors to storms than they did to enemy fire.

Although their heavy long guns and carronades made them more vulnerable to the unpredictable Great Lakes wind and weather, the ships commanded by Chauncey, Yeo, Perry, and Barclay could pack a powerful punch. Their so-called long guns could easily splinter the planking of an enemy ship at distances of half a mile or more. However, most lake captains preferred the stubby, wide-mouthed carronades more useful when firing broadsides at close range. Some carronades could deliver a huge 32-pound cannonball with enough force to completely crush the hull of an opposing vessel.

defenses at Kingston and by ramping up their shipbuilding efforts. As a result, by early the next year, the naval balance of power on Lake Ontario had begun to shift once more in favor of the British.

The Americans would never again seriously threaten Kingston, and this left the ship-yards on nearby Point Frederick free to launch ever larger and more heavily armed warships. Among the dozen or more fighting ships completed here during the war were the 21-gun sloop *Sir George Prevost*, the 42-gun frigate *Princess Charlotte*, the 56-gun frigate *Prince Regent*, and the 56-gun frigate *Psyche*. With the completion of the giant *St. Lawrence* in the autumn of 1814, this flurry of ship construction finally won the Lake Ontario naval arms race for the British.

Commodore Isaac Chauncey launched his attack on Kingston from the recently established American naval base at Sackets Harbor.

WHAT YOU'LL SEE TODAY

LITTLE REMAINS OF THE ORIGINAL navy dockyards on Point Frederick, which is now the site of Kingston's Royal Military College. Although a number of nineteenth-century structures can be found on the grounds of the college, all were built after the war of 1812.

Among the finest and best known of these venerable buildings is the Stone Frigate built in 1820 to house the masts and rigging of British warships dismantled after the war. The massive walls of Fort Frederick on the tip of the peninsula mostly date from the 1840s. Today college students use Fort Frederick as a place to relax.

Located on a point of land across from Fort Frederick is Fort Henry, the site of gun emplacements intended to defend Kingston and its dockyards from American attacks like the one Chauncey attempted in November 1812. The grand fortifications seen here today date from the 1830s. Now a popular living history museum, Fort Henry National Historic Site informs and entertains visitors with martial parades and music, guided tours, and museum exhibits. Fort Henry is located on County Road 2 just to the east of downtown Kingston. From Highway 401 take County Road 15, and County Road 2 to the fort.

YORK BATTLEFIELD
Toronto, Ontario

AT THE BEGINNING OF 1813 the United States held a slight edge in ships and guns on Lake Ontario, and American military leaders were determined to put that advantage to use. Since Kingston was well protected by a fleet of heavily armed warships and formidable land forces, the Americans decided to attack York instead. A small port located near the western end of the lake, York had a population of little more than 600. It could boast neither the commercial nor the strategic importance of Kingston, but it was the capital of Upper Canada, and this made it a tempting target. Capturing it would provide a badly needed boost in morale, or so it was believed.

During the last week of April, an assault force consisting of 14 armed vessels and transports carrying about 1,700 infantry set sail from Sackets Harbor. The American fleet appeared off York on April 26, and by 10 a.m. the following day had put three regiments ashore a few miles from town. Led by General Zebulon Pike, the Americans then marched toward York's substantial but lightly garrisoned fortress.

To defend the town, British General Roger Sheaffe could field only a few hundred regulars, local militia, and Native American warriors. Although outnumbered three or four to one, Sheaffe's men put up a stiff resistance. However, the heart went out of the British line after an ammunition chest blew up killing 20 or more of the defenders. The rest retreated behind the walls of Fort York, while Pike's troops closed in from the west. Under heavy fire from the American fleet, Sheaffe was convinced that his outmanned garrison could not hold out for long. Consequently, he decided to abandon York and retreat toward Kingston. To deny his enemies

General Henry Dearborn was in overall command of the American forces that captured York in 1813.

access to the fort's valuable ammunition stores, Shaeffe ordered some of his men to remain behind and blow up its well-stocked magazine.

Unaware that most of the British garrison had fled, Pike halted his advance a short distance from the walls of Fort York. He was sitting on a tree stump interrogating a captured British sergeant when the magazine exploded. The blast was so powerful that it could be heard at Fort George on the opposite side of the lake. Earth, timber, and enormous hunks of stone were hurled hundreds of feet into the air. A boulder landed on Pike, killing both the general and the soldier he was questioning. Several dozen other American soldiers were killed by the shock of the explosion and by flying debris. The United States had paid a high price for winning the Battle of York. Total American casualties amounted to approximately 300 while the British lost about 500 killed, wounded, or captured.

Leading the ground assault on York was famed explorer Zebulon Pike, who was killed when the fortress magazine exploded.

The Americans remained in York for nearly a week. Pike had strictly warned his troops to respect the private property of Canadian civilians, but once he was dead, discipline quickly deteriorated. There was widespread looting and burning, and even the buildings housing the Upper Canada legislative assembly were left in smoldering ruins. With these acts of wanton destruction the war entered another, more destructive phase. The burning of York would be recalled bitterly by the British and Canadians when they themselves burned Buffalo and Washington the following year.

Three months after their initial attack on York, the U.S. fleet returned to capture the town once again. This time there was little fighting and no great explosions since the York garrison had marched west to reinforce British positions at Burlington. The Americans arrived on July 31 and departed the following day having captured several boats and cannon and several hundred barrels of flour.

The attacks on York accomplished little of true strategic value for the U.S. cause, but they likely had the effect of stiffening the resolve of the British and Canadians. By the autumn of

Fort York National Historic Site preserves one of the finest collections of 1812-era buildings in Canada.

1813, Fort York had been rebuilt and made stronger than before through the addition of new earthworks and blockhouses. The fort remained in British hands for the rest of the war and continued to be used for military purposes right up until the 1930s.

WHAT YOU'LL SEE TODAY

THE VILLAGE ONCE CALLED YORK survived the war and eventually grew into the great city of Toronto. Historic plaques and markers along the Toronto lakefront and elsewhere in the city recall the important events that took place here and elsewhere during the War of 1812. These include a monument in Victoria Square honoring those who lost their lives defending Canada, a provincial plaque in Coronation Square commemorating the U.S. attacks on York, a stone medallion in St. Lawrence Market celebrating the mighty ship of the line *St. Lawrence,* and a sign near Sunnyside Beach, the landing place of the Americans during their first attack on York. Partly as a result of the fighting here, few of York's original buildings still stand. However, a few of them can be found at Fort York National Historic Site located on Garrison Road. Open to the public most of the year, Fort York offers tours, exhibits, and military demonstrations by the colorful Fort York Guards.

This view of Fort York and the Toronto skyline reflects more than two hundred years of history.

SACKETS HARBOR
Sackets Harbor, New York

THE AMERICANS HAD ONLY ONE useful deepwater harbor on their side of Lake Ontario. That was Sackets Harbor, which unlike Kingston, was remote and barely accessible by land. Even so, Sackets Harbor served as a primary U.S. naval base throughout the war, and all of the key American fighting ships that served on the lake were built here.

Because of its considerable importance to the U.S. war effort, Sackets Harbor was under constant threat of attack by the British. A Provincial Marine squadron paid the base an unwelcome visit during the early weeks of the war, arriving off Sackets Harbor on July 19, 1812. Aiming to destroy the *Onieda,* four British warships trapped the American flagship inside the harbor and opened fire on her. However, the British vessels were armed mostly with short-range carronades and they were soon driven off by the long guns of the Americans.

Ten months later the British launched a more determined assault. Having learned that the American fleet and most of the Sackets Harbor garrison had sailed to the western end of the lake for an attack on Fort George, British commanders at Kingston decided to mount an attack of their own upon the most important U.S. military asset in this theater. On May 29, 1813 a powerful fleet under Commodore Yeo swooped down on Sackets Harbor and landed an assault force of nearly 900 troops. Their objective was nothing less than the complete destruction of the base including its vital shipyards.

To defend the base, General Jacob Brown could muster only 400 regulars and a few hundred poorly trained militia. The British flat-bottom landing boats pulled ashore on sandy Horse Island, which was connected to the mainland by shallows. Forming up their regiments, the British fixed bayonets and splashed through the cold lake water toward Brown's hastily organized defensive lines. Combined with punishing cannon fire from Yeo's fleet, the sight of the bayonets proved too much for the Americans who turned and ran. Brown eventually rallied them and together with the steadfast regulars conducted a fighting retreat all the way back to Sackets Harbor.

Believing that the battle was lost, a young American naval officer ordered the military storehouses in Sackets Harbor to be set on fire together with the *General Pike,* a large warship then under construction in the shipyard. The sight of the smoke and flames may have stiffened the resolve of the American defenders, for at this point, the British themselves began to waiver. Soon they were retreating back toward Horse Island where Prevost ordered them aboard the British transports. An unfavorable wind had prevented Yeo's ships from providing effective covering fire for the British attackers. Believing the weather was unlikely to improve, Prevost called off the attack having lost 265 men.

Brown lost about 300 of his regulars and militia but could claim with some justification to have won the Battle of Sackets Harbor.

North Wind Picture Archives

In time the burned military stores were replaced and the severely damaged *General Pike* was repaired and launched to serve with Chauncey's fleet. Even so, the battle had dealt the Americans a debilitating and perhaps decisive blow. Fearing that his base of operations might once again come under attack, Chauncey lost the aggressive spirit that had carried him into Kingston Harbor the previous year. He became increasingly reluctant to participate in amphibious operations or to support the army by carrying supplies for campaigns on land. This would have an especially telling effect during the summer of 1814 when Brown seemed on the verge of driving the British out of the Niagara region.

General Jacob Brown hastily organized American defenses at Sackets Harbor and with some difficulty managed to drive off the British.

WHAT YOU'LL SEE TODAY

NEW YORK MAINTAINS SACKETS HARBOR BATTLEFIELD as a state park and historic site. Visitors can tour the restored navy yard and commandant's house and hike the mile-long history trail. Signs and exhibits along the trail recall the dramatic events that took place here two centuries ago. Especially evocative is the magnificent Memorial Grove and granite 1812 Monument, both of which honor the troops and sailors who served here during the war. The monument was dedicated on May 29, 1913, the centennial anniversary of the battle. The keynote address at the dedication ceremonies was delivered by Franklin Delano Roosevelt, who was then Assistant Secretary of the Navy but would later serve more than 12 years as President.

On Route 75 just outside Sackets Harbor is a monument commemorating the Carrying of the Cable, one of the war's most bizarre and astonishing feats. During the late spring of 1814, marauding British warships drove a U.S. supply convoy ashore near Sandy Creek. Aboard one of the stranded transports was a nine-ton cable needed for construction of a large frigate at Sackets Harbor. Forced to transport the enormous cable overland, the Americans searched diligently but were unable to find a wagon capable of hauling such a load. Instead the cable was carried many miles on the shoulders of 200 footsore volunteers and successfully delivered to the shipyard.

FORT ONTARIO
Oswego, New York

DURING THE WAR OF 1812, the U.S. moved military supplies up through the Mohawk Valley and down the Oswego River to the shores of Lake Ontario. Once they reached the lake, these supplies were stored at Fort Ontario, known today as the port of Oswego, and

Temporary control of eastern Lake Ontario enabled the British to launch a successful amphibious attack on Oswego during the spring of 1814.

then shipped to Sackets Harbor or wherever they were needed. Having played important roles in the French and Indian War and the Revolutionary War, Fort Ontario had once again become a highly strategic asset. Like Sackets Harbor, it would also become the target of a major British attack.

Commodore Yeo had considered an attack during the spring of 1813 but felt his forces were insufficient to overcome Fort Ontario's strong defenses. The following May, however, Yeo was able to catch the fort at a time when it was lightly garrisoned. Fewer than 500 U.S. regulars and militia were on hand to defend the port when a fleet of British warships and transports suddenly appeared offshore on May 5, 1814. Unfavorable winds made it impossible for Yeo's ships to move in close enough to bombard the fort, but by the next morning the weather turned and the attack commenced. Yeo's big frigates, the *Prince Regent* and *Princess Charlotte*, engaged the fort while a cluster of smaller vessels pounded the beaches and nearby woods to clear the way for a landing.

The British troops put ashore at Oswego suffered losses but soon captured Fort Ontario along with large quantities of food and military supplies.

By the middle of the afternoon more than 1,000 British troops were on shore and form-ing up to assault the American lines. Unfortunately for the British, their gunpowder had gotten wet during the landing and most of their muskets could not be fired. As it turned out, however, bayonets combined with cannon fire from Yeo's fleet were enough to rout the defenders. Before long the British had taken the fort, the village of Oswego, and the port's vital storehouses. Captured along with them were 2,400 barrels of food and gunpowder and several small vessels. Among the latter was the 52-ton *Growler,* a five-gun schooner that had already been captured and recaptured three times by the opposing sides.

WHAT YOU'LL SEE TODAY

ADMINISTERED BY THE NEW YORK OFFICE of Parks, Recreation, and Historic Preservation, Fort Ontario is open to the public from May through mid-October. The star-shaped fort seen here today has been restored to its Civil War era appearance. An assort-ment of historic buildings including officers' quarters, barracks, storehouse, and powder magazine have been handsomely restored but none date to the War of 1812. However, parts of the walls and earthworks are more than two centuries old. Fort Ontario is located on East Fourth Street in Oswego on the east bank of the Oswego River.

Soldiers posted along the shores of the Great Lakes or the banks of the St. Lawrence kept a close watch for hostile warships since the sudden appearance of the enemy fleet could bring disaster.

Top heavy with cannon and rigging, oversized warships such as the St. Lawrence *and the* New Orleans *would have been highly vulnerable to the Great Lakes' prodigious storms.*

The Mighty St. Lawrence

With the launching of the HMS *St. Lawrence* at Kingston on September 10, 1814, the naval arms race on Lake Ontario reached its climax. Nearly 200 feet long and with a beam of more than 50 feet, the 2,300-ton *St. Lawrence* was even bigger than the HMS *Victory,* which had served as Admiral Horatio Nelson's flagship at the famed Battle of Trafalgar. The *St. Lawrence* carried a complement of 700 officers and men and mounted 112 guns able to throw nearly a ton of metal in a single broadside. Opposing ships struck by such a ferocious salvo would not just be damaged or sunk—they would be obliterated.

However, the American fleet under Commodore Chauncey had the perfect response to the *St. Lawrence.* Dwarfed by the seemingly invincible British titan, Chauncey's ships took refuge in well-fortified harbors whenever the soaring masts of the *St. Lawrence* appeared on the lake. Meanwhile, the Americans started work on their own super ship, the 110-gun *New Orleans.* As it turned out, the war ended before the *New Orleans* was completed and launched, and the two mighty warships never exchanged broadsides.

Contrary to the expectations of U.S. leaders, Canadians did not rally to the American cause. Instead, they bravely defended their homes. Canada's destiny would be decided at Chateauguay, Crysler's Farm, and other fierce engagements where Canadian militia and First Nations (Native American) warriors stood shoulder to shoulder with British regulars to throw back repeated invasions.

4

St. Lawrence/ Champlain Theater

A MATTER OF MARCHING

FLOWING MORE THAN 600 MILES northeastward to the Atlantic from its entrance near Kingston on Lake Ontario, the St. Lawrence serves as a giant drain for the Great Lakes. A notable tributary of the St. Lawrence is the Richelieu River, which flows from the 110-mile-long Lake Champlain. Missing by only a few miles a link to Lake Champlain and through it to the St. Lawrence, the Hudson River flows 350 miles southward through an ice-and-water scarred valley. All of these prominent geographic features were shaped at least in part by the retreating glaciers of the last ice age, and they in turn have helped shape human history. They played especially important roles in the major conflicts that produced the political geography we know today. Fierce battles were fought over them during the Seven Years (French and Indian) War, during the Revolutionary War, and once again during the War of 1812. In each case, control of these strategic waterways would help determine the outcome of the struggle.

Infantry combat during the War of 1812 required iron discipline. Soldiers often stood so close to the enemy that they could see the faces of the men they were trying to kill—and who were trying to kill them in return.

In 1812, the St. Lawrence Valley became a key objective in an American plan to win the war quickly by seizing Canada. The U.S. invasion plan had three prongs, one of them aimed at Montreal on the St. Lawrence. The march on Montreal was long delayed and in the end never really got underway. Meanwhile, as we have seen, the other two prongs of the American attack—one across the Detroit River far to the west and the other across the Niagara River— failed miserably.

The St. Lawrence was a lifeline for British forces in the Great Lakes region. The river served as the only practical means of bringing in fresh troops and supplies from eastern Canada and from Britain. The Americans made a determined effort to sever this link during the fall of 1813, but their invasion forces were forced back at Chateauguay and Crysler's Farm.

The following year, the British attempted to turn the tables with an invasion of their own. Their thrust was aimed at Lake Champlain and the key American military base at

A year after the failed American attempt to take Montreal, the British launched an invasion of their own. The defeat of their fleet on Lake Champlain forced them to retreat back toward Canada.

Plattsburgh, New York. Capture of this important lake port would give the British control of the lake and threaten the Hudson River Valley beyond. The United States would be forced to capitulate or, at the very least, negotiate a peace from an extremely weak position. But, as it turned out, Plattsburgh did not fall. Its outnumbered and outgunned defenders had one hope, that the small flotilla of armed vessels anchored in the Plattsburgh harbor could somehow hold off a seemingly far more powerful British lake fleet. They succeeded in this and more, and the British invaders had little choice but to retreat.

The British reversal at Plattsburgh would have far-reaching consequences. Together with the failure of the British fleet to hammer its way into Baltimore's Inner Harbor, it would deeply influence the outcome of the peace negotiations in Ghent, Belgium. The Battle of Plattsburgh helped save America just as a year earlier the battles of Chateauguay and Crysler's Farm had saved Canada. When seen from this perspective, the St. Lawrence Theater might be considered the most important and decisive of the war's various arenas of conflict.

OGDENSBURG BATTLEFIELD

Ogdensburg, New York

THE WAR OF 1812 WAS OFTEN very unpopular in communities along the border between Canada and the United States. Typically, the people of these peaceful towns and villages felt less enthusiasm for the war aims of their respective governments than they did kinship for their friends and neighbors just across the border. Even so, they were occasionally caught up in the fighting and forced to pay a high price for decisions that had been made by others.

During the fall of 1812, the people of Ogdensburg, New York found themselves unwillingly thrust onto the frontlines of the war when their town was selected as a strongpoint to be used for harassing British shipping on the St. Lawrence River. Previously, the merchants and farmers of Ogdensburg had carried on a vigorous and sometimes illegal trade with their neighbors in Prescott on the other side of the St. Lawrence. However, the arrival of Captain Benjamin Forsyth in October with a small garrison of U.S. regulars put an end to friendly exchanges between the two towns. Afterward, troops on both sides began to launch raids across the river.

In one such raid during the winter of 1813, the British took several New York militiamen prisoner, locking them up in a jail at Elizabethtown a dozen miles up the river. On February 6,

The raids on Elizabethtown and Ogdensburg took place in the dead of winter.

Forsyth responded by raiding Elizabethtown and releasing the prisoners. He also carried off a small quantity of weapons and supplies and took more than 50 prisoners of his own.

Not surprisingly, Forsyth's raid on Elizabethtown provoked the British who retaliated two weeks later with an attack on Ogdensburg. The British didn't need boats to cross the St. Lawrence, but instead walked across. The river was frozen.

The assault began early on the morning of February 22 as Lt. Colonel George MacDonnell led 600 men, about half of them British regulars and the rest Canadian militia, over the mile-wide jumble of ice that formed the river's surface. Although their field cannon became stuck in the snow, the British soon drove back the Ogdensburg garrison, which had been weakened in order to reinforce American units elsewhere. Seeing that his men were badly outnumbered, Forsyth ordered them to abandon the town and retreat to Sackets Harbor. Once in command of the town, MacDonnell had his troops burn the American barracks and a pair of small schooners that had been ensnared by the river ice. Although a considerable quantity of supplies was confiscated and there was some looting of private property, MacDonnell ordered no official punitive actions against the town or its people.

WHAT YOU'LL SEE TODAY

A WALKING TOUR THAT BEGINS on Water Street in Ogdensburg provides a highly informative overview of the Battle of Ogdensburg. Plaques and signs along the walk describe important events that led to the battle and the fight for Ogdensburg itself. A pamphlet available from the Chamber of Commerce offers additional insight.

At Fort Wellington in Prescott, Ontario, across the St. Lawrence from Ogdensburg, a provincial plaque describes the battle from the Canadian point of view. Consisting primarily of earthworks and timber palisades, Fort Wellington played an important role in the war by serving as an obstacle to American movements along the river. The fort has been meticulously restored and is now a popular destination for travelers interested in Canadian history and the War of 1812. Located beside the river on VanKoughnet Street, Fort Wellington National Historic Park is open daily from Victoria Day in mid-May through September 6.

CHATEAUGUAY BATTLEFIELD

Ormstown, Quebec

AS THE AUTUMN OF 1813 APPROACHED, American military leaders decided to shift the focus of their attention from the western end of Lake Ontario toward the east. Most of the troops that had been used to attack York and capture Fort George were shifted to the eastern end of the lake in preparation for an assault either on Kingston or on Montreal. General James Wilkinson, commander of the American army stationed at Sackets Harbor, preferred making Kingston the primary objective of the campaign, but Secretary of War John Armstrong overruled him. Montreal would be the target, and to capture this important commercial and administrative center, Armstrong set in motion two sizeable columns. One would be led by Wilkinson and descend the St. Lawrence to the western gates of the city. The other, under the command of General Wade Hampton, would march northward from Vermont and attack Montreal from across the St. Lawrence.

The Battle of Chateauguay was fought in heavily forested terrain along the Chateauguay River. There an outnumbered force of mostly French-speaking militia led by Colonel Charles de Salaberry blocked an American attempt to approach Montreal from the south.

Hampton started from Burlington in mid-September with about 5,400 men, but his advance was hampered by poor roads and a severe drought that had dried up most sources of fresh water along his route. It took him more than a month to reach British defensive positions along the banks of the Chateauguay River south of Montreal. By this time his force had been reduced to fewer than 4,000 by the refusal of many militiamen to cross into Canada.

General Wade Hampton commanded American forces at the Battle of Chateauguay in 1813. Having failed to break through British lines, Hampton retreated to Plattsburgh.

Arrayed against Hampton's diminished force were about 1,700 Canadian regulars, militia, and Indians under the command of Colonel Charles de Salaberry. To make his stand, Salaberry chose a position along the edge of a forest with one end anchored on a ford across the Chateauguay. On October 25, Hampton attempted to dislodge Salaberry by sending about half his troops across the river for a flanking attack on the ford. Rather blindly led by Colonel Robert Purdy, however, this detachment soon became hopelessly lost in the dark. Purdy and his men only discovered their whereabouts late the next day when, seemingly by accident, they bumped into the troops Salaberry had posted on the far side of the river to guard the ford. Instead of attacking the ford, Purdy was himself

French-Canadian by birth, Salaberry had served in the British Army since 1792.

attacked as troops on both sides of the river opened a brisk fire on his exhausted infantry. Purdy and his men were soon driven back into the wilds.

Meanwhile, Hampton had launched an assault on the British lines in front of the forest. This effort proved no more successful than Purdy's flanking maneuver, and Hampton soon called off the attack. That same evening Hampton met with his senior officers and decided to retreat back across the border.

Wilkinson had still not advanced beyond Ogdensburg when he received word of Hampton's retreat. Having

Among the least capable of the men who led American troops during the War of 1812, General James Wilkinson was relieved of command after a bungled invasion of Canada in 1813.

been placed in overall command of the campaign, Wilkinson ordered Hampton to turn about and join forces with him on the St. Lawrence. Hampton openly despised Wilkinson and rejected the order out of hand. He and his men kept going until they reached Plattsburgh, and soon afterward Hampton resigned his command.

Considering the importance of the battle and the number of troops involved, casualties at Chateauguay were extremely light. Hampton lost about 65 killed and wounded while Salaberry's militia suffered only two killed and 16 wounded. Although losses were minimal, Hampton's failure at Chateauguay was yet another embarrassing setback for the Americans. At the same time Salaberry's success gave the British and Canadians a significant boost in morale. Having held the line against superior numbers at Chateauguay, they could now concentrate on halting Wilkinson's push down the St. Lawrence.

It is worth noting that Salaberry won the Battle of Chateauguay with a force consisting primarily of Canadian militia. Many were French speakers, but many others were of English, Scottish, Irish, or other English-speaking lineage. Canadians remember and celebrate this battle as an early instance of close, patriotic cooperation between Canadians of diverse heritages.

WHAT YOU'LL SEE TODAY

OPERATED BY PARKS CANADA, the Chateauguay Battlefield National Historic Site is located just off Route 138 about 28 miles southwest of Montreal. The wild lands and forests present here in 1813 have long since given way to verdant farm fields. However, the park visitor center is filled with exhibits and displays that help visitors visualize the important events that took place at Chateauguay two centuries ago. An impressive monument dedicated during the late nineteenth century marks the site of the barricade that protected the main British line.

CRYSLER'S FARM BATTLEFIELD
Morrisburg, Ontario

DESPITE THE DEFEAT OF HAMPTON'S forces at Chateauguay and the looming onset of winter, General Wilkinson still hoped to capture Montreal. In command of a substantial force of 8,000 infantry, 24 guns, and more than 150 gunboats and transports, he began his advance down the St. Lawrence in early November. Having bypassed Kingston, he then slipped past Prescott without engaging the formidable British guns and garrison at Fort Wellington. His soldiers were put ashore above Ogdensburg while the U.S. fleet ran past the fort in the night. The troops then marched along the south bank of the river to re-board their transports downriver safely beyond the reach of the Fort Wellington artillery.

At Crysler's Farm on the banks of the St. Lawrence River, a small force of British regulars under Lieutenant Colonel Joseph Morrison defeated a much larger U.S. detachment led by General John Boyd. Here devoted War of 1812 buffs re-enact this two-hundred-year-old battle.

This deft maneuver seemed to open the way to Montreal, but Wilkinson was about to receive a shock. On November 10 he learned that a sizeable British detachment had been pursuing him for several days. The British force on his heels consisted of a mixed force of approximately 900 British and Canadian regulars, militia, and Iroquois. They were commanded by Colonel Joseph Morrison, who had been ordered to follow Wilkinson's army as closely as possible and harass it at every opportunity.

To deal with this threat to the rear, Wilkinson moved most of his troops to the north side of the river landing them just above the treacherous Long Sault Rapids. There he designated Brigadier General John Boyd to lead an assault on Morrison's infantry. On November 11, Boyd and approximately 2,500 U.S. regulars marched upriver toward the British, who were arrayed in a series of broad, open fields belonging to a farmer named John Crysler.

The two sides crashed into one another about the middle of the afternoon, and the British quickly got the better of the fighting. Although outnumbered by more than two to one, the British flanks were protected by woods and marshy ground that made it difficult for the Americans to maneuver. Effective musket and cannon fire from Morrison's better disciplined and more experienced troops threw back one American assault after another, and by nightfall Boyd had ordered his men to fall back. So demoralized were Boyd's troops that they boarded their transports and fled back across the river onto U.S. soil.

Morrison's victory had been won at a cost of fewer than 200 killed, wounded, or missing in action. Wilkinson's army had lost more than 450 men, but the loss to the American cause was even greater than the casualty list would indicate. On the day after the battle, Wilkinson recalled General Jacob Brown and the brigade of troops he had earlier sent eastward to clear the roads to Montreal. Soon afterward Wilkinson learned that General Hampton, who had been defeated in late October at the Battle of Chateauguay, was refusing to join him for a final push on Montreal. Short of supplies and with no support coming from Hampton, a dispirited Wilkinson felt he had no choice but to abandon the campaign.

With the failure of the Montreal campaign, the United States may have lost its last realistic chance to win the war. Had Wilkinson and others managed to seize a substantial portion of Upper Canada in 1813, Britain might have been forced to negotiate a peace highly favorable to the Americans. This opportunity would no longer exist in 1814 after Napoleon had been driven from power, freeing large numbers of British ships and troops for the struggle in North America.

The Battle of Crysler's Farm is considered an epic event in Canadian history, since here British regulars stood shoulder to shoulder with Canadians of both French- and English-speaking heritage as well as Native warriors to turn back a foreign threat. In the United States, the invasion was forgotten as quickly as possible, but in Canada it would be remembered forever.

WHAT YOU'LL SEE TODAY

THE BATTLEFIELD WHERE Colonel Morrison's outnumbered regulars and militia turned back an American invasion has been all but destroyed by time and progress. When the St. Lawrence Seaway was constructed during the 1950s, much of the battlefield was cut away to make a channel for large, seagoing ships. Soil from the battlefield was piled into a large mound not far from the original site of the fighting. Flanked by a pair of 24-pound cannon, an impressive pyramidal granite monument commemorating the British/Canadian victory stands atop the mound. Nearby is the Battle Memorial Building, which houses battlefield artifacts and a mural depicting the encounter. The mound and memorial building are located near Upper Canada Village on Highway 2 a few miles east of Morrisburg.

BATTLE OF LACOLLE MILLS
Lacolle, Quebec

IN LATE MARCH 1814 General Wilkinson moved once more in the direction of Montreal. Leaving behind the army's winter quarters at Plattsburgh, Wilkinson and 4,000 men marched north along the shores of Lake Champlain and the banks of the Richelieu River. With a force barely half the size of the one he had led down the St. Lawrence five months earlier, Wilkinson could not hope to breech Montreal's defenses, which were stronger now than they had been the previous autumn. However, he believed this maneuver might distract the British and draw valuable troops from other theaters. He also thought that a victory over the enemy, even a relatively small and strategically insignificant one, might restore his military career, which had been on the wane since his defeat at Crysler's Farm in November.

As his target, Wilkinson selected a British position on Lacolle Creek a few miles north of the border. The defenses here guarded nothing of any real value. But from Wilkinson's point of view this place had two considerable advantages as an objective: it was on Canadian soil, and he seemed very likely to win here. Fewer than 200 regulars manned the British line, which was anchored by an old stone mill and a Revolutionary War blockhouse.

Wilkinson launched his attack on the mill and blockhouse at about 3 p.m. on March 30. His gunners opened fire with three small cannon, but they made almost no impression on the thick timber walls of the buildings. So long as these protective structures remained intact, an infantry attack seemed unlikely to succeed, and after about two hours, the Americans began to run short on ammunition. Meanwhile, the British defenders were reinforced by several hundred men drawn from small garrisons downriver.

The muskets used by War of 1812 infantry produced a great deal of smoke and noise but were very inaccurate. If a heavy lead musket ball struck an opponent, however, it would almost certainly kill him.

Although still heavily outnumbered, the British were emboldened by the seeming ineptitude of the Americans, so much so that they attempted to storm the U.S. artillery emplacements. The assault on the guns was driven back, but it unnerved Wilkinson's men. So, too, did the continuous fire from British gunboats in the river and from the Congreve rockets that occasionally streaked in their direction. Seeing that his attack had failed, Wilkinson ordered a retreat back to Plattsburgh. Upon his return, Wilkinson learned that he had already been relieved of command. A year later he would stand before a military tribunal in Washington to face charges of misconduct. Although acquitted, Wilkinson never returned to duty.

WHAT YOU'LL SEE TODAY

BUILT IN 1781, THE LACOLLE BLOCKHOUSE still stands. Located off Route 221, it is administered by the government of Quebec as a historic site. A plaque near the blockhouse describes the battle.

BATTLE OF PLATTSBURGH/LAKE CHAMPLAIN
Plattsburgh, New York

FOLLOWING NAPOLEON'S ABDICATION in 1814, the British resolved to bring a swift end to the war with the United States, and they now had the resources to do it. Troops and ships no longer needed for the war with France were sent to North America, where they tightened the blockade of the U.S. coast and prepared for a series of land campaigns aimed at forcing the Americans to capitulate. Among the most important of these thrusts would be a drive southward along the shores of Lake Champlain and, perhaps, into the Hudson River Valley beyond. A similar invasion attempted during the Revolutionary War had ended disastrously with the defeat of General John Burgoyne at the Battle of Saratoga, but the British were determined not to fail this time. To make sure the invasion succeeded, General George Prevost, the Governor of Upper Canada and commander in chief of all the British forces stationed there, would lead it himself.

General George Prevost served as overall commander of British forces in North America.

At the end of August, Prevost marched south at the head of an army of 11,000 men. His immediate objective was Plattsburgh, located about one-third of the way down the western shore of Lake Champlain.

Prevost was fortunate in that the Americans had recently weakened the garrison at Plattsburgh. Aware that the British were amassing a sizeable force north of the border, U.S. military leaders guessed incorrectly that it would be used for an attack on Sackets Harbor and had recently transferred 4,000 men there from Plattsburgh. This left General Alexander Macomb with only 1,500 regulars and about 2,000 hastily mustered militia from New York and Vermont to man the Plattsburgh defenses.

During the late summer of 1814, General Prevost advanced toward Plattsburgh with a sizeable force of 11,000 men. His army depended heavily on water transport for supplies.

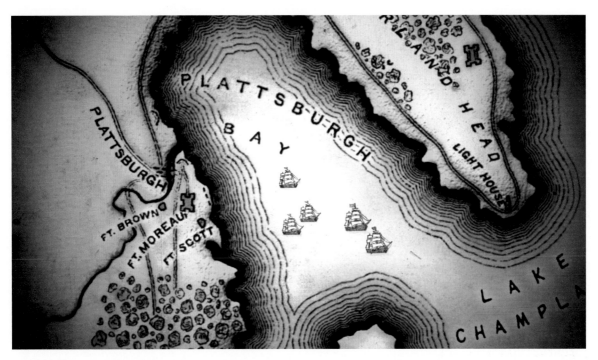

Guarding the western shore of Lake Champlain and the route to Albany, Plattsburgh was the most important American military base in northern New York. The U.S. fleet anchored in Plattsburgh Bay proved the key to its defense.

Having learned to his horror that Prevost was, in fact, heading for Plattsburgh rather than Sackets Harbor, Macomb sent several hundred of his men north in an attempt to slow the British advance. They burned bridges, erected roadblocks, and did whatever they could to harass the invading army. Despite their best efforts, however, Prevost's brigades appeared just outside Plattsburgh on September 6. Meanwhile, the depleted American garrison prepared to make a stand along the south bank of the Saranac River.

Prevost did not order an immediate all-out assault on Plattsburgh's defenses. If he had done so, the poorly prepared Americans would likely have been overwhelmed, and this in turn might very well have changed the course of history. However, the planks had been removed from the bridges across the Saranac, and the British had trouble finding a suitable ford. As a result, Prevost decided to put off a major attack for several days. He saw in this the advantage of giving Captain George Downie time to reach Plattsburgh with the powerful British lake fleet and destroy the American warships riding at anchor in the harbor.

For the previous two years British and American shipbuilders on Lake Champlain had been caught up in their own miniature version of the separate naval arms races that had taken place on Lakes Ontario and Erie. The British had every reason to believe they had won the competition for naval supremacy on Lake Champlain once and for all by launching the 1,200-ton, 37-gun frigate *Confiance,* a vessel nearly twice the size of the largest American warship on the lake. Unfortunately for Prevost, the *Confiance* was not ready to sail when his army crossed the border into New York, and Downie's fleet did not appear off Plattsburgh until September 9.

With the fleet finally on hand to support him, Prevost scheduled his attack for September 11. The fighting on land and in the harbor was to begin simultaneously. That way the gunners on the American ships could not assist their outnumbered comrades on shore. Prevost intended to outflank the Plattsburgh defenses by sending General Frederick Robinson with a large detachment of troops across a ford about 3 miles to the north. Meanwhile, his artillery would silence Macomb's guns and a feint attack on the partially dismantled bridges would distract the American infantry.

Unfortunately for the British, none of this unfolded as Prevost had planned. The land assault was delayed for more than an hour and so could not be coordinated with the fighting

The British land forces under General Prevost greatly outnumbered the Americans defending Plattsburgh. However, the battle was decided out on the waters of Lake Champlain, where Lieutenant Thomas Macdonough's squadron defeated the British fleet.

out in Plattsburgh Bay. In the artillery duel that was supposed to knock out Macomb's cannon, the Americans gave as good as they got and even began to gain the upper hand toward the end of the battle. The British assault on the bridges that was supposed to distract the Americans was easily repulsed and failed to deceive anyone, least of all Macomb. The U.S. commander fully expected a flanking maneuver and was ready to meet it, but as it turned out, the main British attack never materialized. Robinson's detachment got lost, and it was the middle of the day before his troops reached the ford, which they found well-defended by American riflemen. Just as Robinson's men were attempting to drive off the defenders and cross the Saranac, Prevost ordered them to retreat, since by that time, the battle had already been lost.

The moment of truth for the battle, the campaign, and perhaps, for the entire war had come at 9 a.m. when Captain Downie's fleet rounded Cumberland Head across from Plattsburgh. Downie had under his command 16 armed vessels including the eleven-gun *Chubb,* the eleven-gun *Finch,* the sixteen-gun *Linnet,* and twelve small gunboats as well as the powerful thirty-seven-gun *Confiance.* Arrayed just inside of Cumberland Head and the mouth of Plattsburgh Bay were fourteen American vessels under the command of Lieutenant Thomas Macdonough. These included the twenty-gun *Eagle,* the seventeen-gun *Ticonderoga,* the seven-gun *Prebble,* and ten gunboats in addition to Macdonough's flagship, the twenty-six-gun *Saratoga.*

Downie had more ships and guns, and many of his cannon had a longer range than the stubby carronades of the American fleet. With these long guns, Downie thought he would be able to cruise just beyond the reach of the enemy artillery and pound the American fleet to splinters. However, Macdonough had unexpectedly ordered his fleet to remain at anchor, forcing the British to enter Plattsburgh Bay and fight at close quarters. Remaining at anchor gave the American ships another considerable advantage. When one side of the ship was battered to splinters by enemy artillery, the anchors could be used to turn the vessels around so that another broadside could be fired using the cannon on the other side. In this way, the Americans were able to outgun and disable the larger British fighting ships, which, one by one, surrendered. The mighty *Confiance* had surrendered after a little more than an hour of fighting. Captain Downie did not live to see his proud flagship strike her colors for he had been killed by one of the first shots fired in what has come to be called the Battle of Lake Champlain.

With Downie's fleet gone and the Americans in near total command of the lake, Prevost recognized that his invasion of the United States was now a lost cause. The British soon withdrew to the north, leaving their encampment so stealthily that they were almost a day's march away before Macomb realized they had left. Heavy rains had begun to pour, and no doubt wisely, Macomb decided not to pursue them.

Securely anchored in Plattsburgh Bay, Macdonough's ships pounded the British vessels into submission. Prevost—with his fleet gone and his supply lines threatened—had little choice but to retreat.

In addition to their losses in ships, the British lost about 700 killed, wounded, or captured. American casualties amounted to 220 men. However, the damage done to the opposing military forces was slight compared to the strategic and political consequences of the battle. American morale had seemed on the point of crumbling, but now it stiffened once again. Instead of being able to dictate the terms of peace, the British were forced to negotiate on an equal basis with the Americans.

WHAT YOU'LL SEE TODAY

NEITHER THE TOWN OF PLATTSBURGH nor the surrounding country look much like they did in the early nineteenth century. However, the Battle of Plattsburgh Interpretive Center makes it easy to imagine the Plattsburgh of 1814 and the key events that took place there. Located on Washington Road, this exceptional historical museum offers an interactive diorama, scale models of the ships that fought in the Battle of Lake Champlain, and famous paintings that depict the action on both land and water. Plaques along the Saranac River and in front of historic local homes recall the siege and defense of Plattsburgh. A series of grassy mounds just off Route 9 are all that remains of Fort Brown, most important of the defensive works that helped U.S. forces stop the British. Near the Plattsburgh City Hall is the Macdonough Victory Monument. A 135-foot limestone obelisk, the monument features carvings of Macdonough's four largest vessels. Those and other fighting ships in the American fleet were constructed near Vergennes, Vermont, about 40 miles south of Plattsburgh. Today a stone monument stands on the site of the Vergennes Shipyard where these historic vessels were built.

Steeped in maritime tradition, New England, Nova Scotia, and New Brunswick provided ships and sailors for the war at sea. However, these northeastern states and provinces saw little or no land combat.

5
Northeast Theater
QUIET CORNER

COASTAL COMMUNITIES IN THE northeastern United States and Canada were mostly spared the violence and destruction that the War of 1812 heaped upon many other parts of North America. There was little or no land combat in New England, New Brunswick, or Nova Scotia. Either lukewarm or openly opposed to the war from the first, New Englanders were extremely reluctant to take up arms against their neighbors across the border, and while coastal Canadians remained steadfastly loyal to the crown, the fighting on land never really reached them. However, these traditionally maritime peoples were very much affected and threatened by the naval war.

Blockades of American ports such as Boston, Portland, and Portsmouth depressed the economy of the northeastern U.S. while the threat of enemy raids caused New Englanders to fortify harbors and river entrances. Though less vulnerable to attack than American ports, St. Andrews, Halifax, Saint John, and other Canadian coastal towns and cities built new fortifications or strengthened existing ones. Meanwhile, sailors from both sides of the border fought on the high seas either aboard regular naval vessels or as privateers.

FAST FRIGATES

WITH ONLY HALF A DOZEN or so fighting ships of modest size, the U.S. Navy never had the slightest hope of wresting control of the seas from the Royal Navy. The British possessed nearly 1,000 warships, more than a few of which were ships-of-the-line, what today we would call battleships. Overwhelmingly outnumbered and outgunned, the Americans opted for what is sometimes described as an "asymmetrical" strategy. They employed their meager naval resources in the most efficient way possible, using them to strike the British where they were most vulnerable—along their long, lightly patrolled trade routes.

The tiny U.S. fleet aimed to capture or destroy as many British freighters and supply ships as possible while avoiding superior enemy warships. Whenever confronted by larger, more powerful opponents, the fast American frigates made a run for it, and they nearly always escaped unscathed. On the other hand, if they had a chance to take on an individual British warship upon more or less even terms, they were prepared to fight. Just such an engagement took place early in the war.

The USS Constitution *and other American frigates carried as many as fifty guns and could crush the hull of an enemy ship with a single blazing broadside consisting of nearly half a ton of metal.*

In mid-August 1812 the USS *Constitution,* under the command of Captain Isaac Hull, was patrolling the Atlantic several hundred miles east of Boston and southeast of Halifax, Nova Scotia. About the middle of the afternoon on August 19, Hull's lookouts sighted an enemy ship that turned out to be the HMS *Guerrière,* a British frigate. The *Guerrière* fired two ineffective broadsides from extreme range and then attempted to sail away. The speedy *Constitution* soon overhauled the British vessel, pulled abeam, and fired a devastating broadside that brought down one of the *Guerrière's* masts and severely damaged another. This enabled the *Constitution* to draw ahead and cross her opponent's bow. Within half an hour the *Guerrière* had been shot to splinters, and Captain J.R. Dacres was forced to haul down his colors and surrender his ship. The *Guerrière* was so badly damaged that the Americans could not haul it back to port as a prize. Instead, it was burned as a useless hulk. It was in this battle that the *Constitution* earned her famous nickname "Old Ironsides" when the British gunners found they could not penetrate her hull.

One of the most famous naval confrontations of the war took place in August 1812 when the frigates Constitution *and* Guerrière *sighted one another several hundred miles east of Boston and opened fire. The* Constitution *eventually overwhelmed the more lightly armed British vessel.*

Word of the *Guerrière's* demise struck the British admiralty like a thunderbolt. So, too, did news of American victories in several similar frigate-versus-frigate sea battles. One of these came in October when the USS *United States* took on the British frigate *Macedonian* off Madeira in the Azores. Although the British vessel held the advantage of a windward position, the more heavily armored American frigate knocked down the *Macedonian's* masts and punched more than 100 holes in her hull before forcing her to surrender.

This colorful illustration published in 1898 shows the deck of the Constitution *and Captain Hull looking through a telescope, perhaps at the moment he first sighted the* Guerrière.

A few days after Christmas, the *Constitution* was at it again, this time off the coast of Brazil. In one of the most fiercely contested sea duels ever fought, she destroyed the British frigate *Java* in a three-hour slugfest. All of *Java's* senior officers and nearly half her crew were killed or wounded, many of them by marine riflemen stationed in the *Constitution's* rigging.

It had become obvious to Royal Navy admirals that they were up against an entirely new sort of foe. They had never before encountered anything quite like the American frigates. These well-constructed vessels were faster and carried more guns than most British frigates, and they had sturdier hulls made of dense oak planking that was difficult to penetrate with cannon shot. In most cases, though few in Britain were prepared to admit it, the U.S. frigates were also better served by their officers and crews than their Royal Navy counterparts. To avoid future embarrassments, the admiralty ordered its frigate captains to avoid taking on the tough American frigates unless they had a clear advantage or assistance from other Royal Navy vessels.

Early U.S. successes at sea helped raise the morale of Americans who had been shaken by repeated defeats on land. They also forced Britain and other European countries to take the upstart Americans more seriously. After the first year of the war, however, there would be very few U.S. naval victories on the high seas. The huge British fleet managed to bottle up most of the U.S. frigates in their home ports or to outgun and defeat them when they attempted to break through the blockade.

Late in 1812 the Constitution *won another lopsided victory, this time over the British frigate* Java. *The latter vessel was too badly damaged to be salvaged.*

DON'T GIVE UP THE SHIP

IRONICALLY, THE FIRST OF THE American frigates to be lost was the very same vessel that had been on the losing end of the notorious confrontation between the USS *Chesapeake* and the HMS *Leopard* in 1807. The unlucky *Chesapeake* would tangle with another British frigate in the waters off Boston on June 1, 1813. Aware that the British frigate *Shannon* was waiting just outside the harbor, Captain James Lawrence ordered the *Chesapeake* to sea. At about 5 p.m., the two vessels sighted one another, exchanged broadsides, and then came to close quarters. Mortally wounded by musket fire, Lawrence issued his final order. "Don't give up the ship," he said. "Fight her till she sinks."

A boarding party from the British warship Shannon *overpowers the crew of* Chesapeake. *Although Captain James Lawrence's last words were "Don't give up the ship," that's exactly what his men had to do.*

However, a British boarding party soon overwhelmed the American crew and captured the *Chesapeake*. She was taken to Halifax as a prize and later served with distinction in the Royal Navy. Eventually, she was broken up and her timbers used to build a mill in Wickham, England. Known as the Chesapeake Mill, it still stands.

HALIFAX DEFENSES
Halifax, Nova Scotia

AS THE MOST IMPORTANT British-held seaport in North America, Halifax was well defended even before the outbreak of war with the United States. Its defenses included Fort George, an earth-and-stone redoubt located on a hill dominating the town and harbor as well as a massive fortified tower and extensive gun emplacements. During the war, the British protected Halifax with a powerful fleet and a large garrison. Perhaps not surprisingly, the harbor and the thriving city that had grown up beside it were never seriously threatened.

WHAT YOU'LL SEE TODAY

MOST OF THE DEFENSIVE STRUCTURES that stood here during the War of 1812 have been substantially altered and look nothing like they did then. Fort George, known today as the Halifax Citadel, was greatly expanded during the 1860s and its walls given the star-shaped battlements typical of nineteenth-century forts. Located within easy walking distance of the Halifax waterfront, the fort is now part of the Halifax Citadel National Historic Site. During warm-weather months, uniformed re-enactors give visitors a sense of what life was like for soldiers stationed here in earlier times. Other important fortifications can be seen on St. George's Island, a sizeable glacial drumlin located out in the harbor. The historical structures on the island are maintained by Parks Canada. They can be seen from shore, but are not currently open to the public.

About 8 miles south of town is the York Redoubt National Historic Site. A gun emplacement here defended Halifax against attack from the sea.

St. Paul's Church and Cemetery on Barrington Street has several memorials and gravestones related to the war. General Robert Ross, killed during the unsuccessful British assault on Baltimore, is buried here. On display on the grounds of Government House is a long gun from the HMS *Shannon,* victor of the famous ship-versus-ship duel with the USS *Chesapeake.*

ST. ANDREWS BLOCKHOUSE
St. Andrews, New Brunswick

WHEN WAR WITH THE UNITED STATES loomed, the British began to fortify border areas of New Brunswick with heavy timber blockhouses. Protected by walls often several feet thick, the soldiers inside the blockhouses could fire at attacking troops through small gun ports and windows. The blockhouses were vulnerable to heavy artillery but could stand up indefinitely to small field cannon and musket fire. New Brunswick and its blockhouses were never seriously threatened by American attack during the war.

WHAT YOU'LL SEE TODAY

OF THE DOZEN OR SO BLOCKHOUSES that helped defend New Brunswick during the War of 1812, only one remains standing. Located on Joe's Point Road along the waterfront in St. Andrews, it is administered by Parks Canada as the St. Andrews Blockhouse National Historic Site. The blockhouse is open to the public during the summer.

CARLETON MARTELLO TOWER
Saint John, New Brunswick

AT SAINT JOHN, NEW BRUNSWICK, the British built a Martello tower to help defend this strategic port city. The tower stood on a hill where it commanded a 360-degree view of the harbor, town, and surrounding countryside. The war was already over by the time the tower was completed, but as things turned out, it was never needed. New Brunswick was in a relatively quiet sector, and the Americans never threatened the town.

Martello towers—circular structures with thick stone walls and guns at the top—were an early version of the pillboxes and other "hardened" defensive structures that would play such an important role in the world wars of the twentieth century. Capable of slowing or stopping an enemy assault, they served much the same function as a blockhouse but were much stronger and more durable. The Saint John tower was intended to be part of an extensive defensive complex with walls and earthen entrenchments, but only the tower was completed.

WHAT YOU'LL SEE TODAY

A FAMILIAR AND MUCH-LOVED Saint John landmark, the Carleton Martello Tower has been designated a national historic site. The tower is located just south of Highway 1 in West Saint John. Open to the public during warm-weather months, it offers a grand view of the city and the Bay of Fundy.

In October 1812 the frigate United States *battled the British frigate* Macedonian *off the Azores.*

FORT GEORGE
Castine, Maine

IN SEPTEMBER 1814, BRITISH TROOPS occupied Fort George and Fort Madison in the strategically placed town of Castine. Fort George had been an important British military base during the Revolutionary War and had withstood an unsuccessful attack by Continental forces under Samuel Lovell and Paul Revere in 1779. The British not only managed to hold the town but also destroyed the Continental army and fleet that had been sent against them. Perhaps the memory of that military disaster, which had taken place a generation earlier, made the Americans extremely reluctant to challenge the British once they had established a strongly fortified position at Castine. At one point Fort George bristled with more than sixty British cannon. British forces remained here until the spring of 1815, some months after the war had ended.

WHAT YOU'LL SEE TODAY

Only crude earthworks remain of Forts George and Madison. However, the town itself is highly evocative of the 1812 era and features numerous eighteenth- and early nineteenth-century houses. Among them are several structures pressed into service as barracks, offices, and warehouses during the British occupation. Castine can be reached from Highway 1 by way of Routes 175 and 166.

Another Maine military post captured by the British during the war was Fort O'Brian near Machiasport, about 100 miles to the east of Castine. The British attack was a serious affair involving about 900 troops who easily drove off the small garrison at Fort O'Brian. Having burned the fort and removed its cannon, the British soon departed. The action here is recalled by a plaque as well as restored earthworks and cannon.

Other restored 1812-era Maine forts can be seen at Wiscasset on Highway 1 well to the west of Castine and at Kittery near the New Hampshire border. Like most other forts in the northeastern U.S. and Canada, Wiscasset's Fort Edgecomb was never threatened during the war. However, the fort's reconstructed octagonal blockhouse and palisade recall the era as does the exquisite coastal village it was intended to protect. Fort McClary in Kittery was used in several wars including the Revolutionary War and War of 1812. Administered by the Maine Department of Parks and Recreation, the site now consists of a blockhouse, powder magazine, and other historic structures open to the public.

FORT CONSTITUTION
Portsmouth, New Hampshire

ORIGINALLY KNOWN AS FORT WILLIAM and Mary, the sturdy, brick-walled fortification at the entrance to the key harbor at Portsmouth, New Hampshire, played an important role in the Revolutionary War. In 1775 a colonial raiding party seized the fort and carried off five tons of gunpowder and some light cannon. The gunpowder would prove extremely helpful to the Patriot cause during the early months of the conflict. When war with Britain threatened once again early in the nineteenth century, the U.S. government rebuilt the fort, greatly increasing the size and strength of its brick walls. In 1808, it was given a new and more patriotic name—Fort Constitution. Even though it was garrisoned during the War of 1812, Fort Constitution was never attacked.

WHAT YOU'LL SEE TODAY

WHILE IT SAW NO COMBAT during the War of 1812, Fort Constitution is haunted by history and well worth a visit. The stout walls of the old fort are quite impressive as is the adjacent steel cylinder lighthouse tower. The fort is located just off Route 1B near Portsmouth. An interesting way to see the fort and the lighthouse is from the water, a viewpoint made possible during the summer by Portsmouth ferries and harbor cruises.

North Wind Picture Archives

Not all of the war's maritime duels were fought by frigates. In October 1812 the American sloop Wasp *defeated the British sloop* Frolic *in a sea battle near Bermuda.*

USS CONSTITUTION
Boston, Massachusetts

THE NAVAL ACT OF 1794 AUTHORIZED construction of six frigates, one of which was the USS *Constitution*. Named by President George Washington himself, the *Constitution* was launched in 1797. She took part in the war against the Barbary Pirates during the early years of the nineteenth century and by 1812 had become a mainstay of the small U.S. Navy. During the War of 1812, the *Constitution* captured or burned many British merchant ships and defeated five Royal Navy warships, including the *Guerrière, Java, Levant, Pictou,* and *Cyane.*

Shipbuilders gave the *Constitution* thick planking made of a dense coastal oak. As a result, cannonballs often bounced harmlessly off the sides of the tough frigate. While demolishing the *Guerrière* during the fall of 1812 she earned her much beloved nickname "Old Ironsides" when astonished British gunners cried out in frustration that "she has sides of iron."

Today, the *Constitution* remains afloat and is still part of the U.S. Navy. This makes her the oldest commissioned warship in the entire world. It has been two centuries since the *Constitution* fired a shot in anger, but she still has a job to do and does it very well. Her full-time assignment is as a museum ship in Boston Harbor. The frigate is still capable of sailing under her own power, but the last time she did so was 1997.

WHAT YOU'LL SEE TODAY

MAINTAINED BY THE U.S. PARK SERVICE, the *Constitution* is a must-see for anyone visiting Boston, as is the adjacent USS Constitution Museum. The old ship is permanently berthed at the Boston Navy Yard and can be reached by taking one of the Charlestown exits off I-93 in downtown Boston. Navy personnel offer regular tours of the ship, usually from about 10 a.m. until late afternoon. Although Old Ironsides looks much the way she did during her heyday on the high seas, she has been restored and refitted so many times that very few of her original wooden timbers and metal parts remain. However, this is unlikely to diminish the thrill of walking her venerable decks. The nearby museum adds perspective to the history of this great, old fighting ship. Keep in mind that the museum is operated by a separate nonprofit organization and its hours may vary slightly from those of the ship itself.

Still young and nimble during the War of 1812, "Old Ironsides" often made short work of her British opponents. It took her less than two hours to demolish the fine frigate Java, *turning her into a splintered hulk.*

Here the Constitution *tows a prize British vessel captured in February 1815 before the American captain received word that the war was already over.*

FORT PICKERING AND FORT LEE
Salem, Massachusetts

THE BRITISH CHOSE NOT TO ATTACK Salem during the War of 1812, but they might very well have considered it. At that time Salem was one of the busiest and most prosperous ports in America and would have been a tempting target for a Royal Navy raid. No doubt they were discouraged by the powerful cannon of Forts Pickering and Lee that guarded the entrance of Salem Harbor.

A substantial structure of earth and stone, Fort Pickering dates all the way back to the 1600s. Located on the north side of the harbor entrance on Winter Island, the fort had been considerably strengthened to ward off the British. Capping a stretch of high ground about half a mile to the west was a smaller defensive structure known as Fort Lee. A star-shaped earthwork, Fort Lee served as an emplacement for four large guns.

WHAT YOU'LL SEE TODAY

NEITHER FORT LEE NOR FORT PICKERING has been substantially restored, but therein lies part of their attraction. They are of less interest to casual tourists than to history-minded travelers who wish to quietly contemplate two centuries of history. Both historic sites are open to the public year-round.

More heavily trafficked by tourists, especially during the summer, is Salem Maritime National Park, which celebrates Salem's extraordinary centuries-long career as a haven for seafarers. An important feature of the park is Derby Wharf, which was frequented by privateers during the War of 1812. Derby Wharf and the park visitor center are both located on the Salem waterfront.

To the west of Salem in nearby Marblehead, Massachusetts, is historic Fort Sewall. Gunners here helped the USS *Constitution* escape a pair of British frigates that attempted to trap the vessel in the narrows off this coast on April 3, 1814. The fort is now a public park.

CASTLE CLINTON AND FORT WOOD

New York City, New York

DURING THE EARLY 1800s, New York City was one of the busiest ports in North America, if not the entire world. This made it an obvious target for an attack by Royal Navy ships or an amphibious assault by British troops. To protect the city and its vital harbor, the U.S. government built a series of fortifications on the southern end of Manhattan Island. Among these was a circular sandstone battery that eventually came to be called Castle Clinton in honor of DeWitt Clinton, who was mayor of New York City at the time of the war and later became governor of New York. The battery mounted more than two dozen powerful guns, which served as a considerable deterrent to naval attack by way of the Hudson.

Another important defensive structure was Fort Wood, located on what is known today as Liberty Island. The star-shaped stone fort had eleven pointed bastions that opened would-be attackers to a deadly crossfire. Combined with the artillery on Manhattan Island, Fort Wood's twenty-four large guns were prepared to place enemy ships in a crossfire as well. Fort Wood, Castle Clinton, and other fortifications guarding the harbor entrance were so formidable that the British never attempted to attack New York.

WHAT YOU'LL SEE TODAY

LOCATED IN BATTERY PARK on the lower end of Manhattan Island, Castle Clinton is now a national monument. The old fort has a long and diverse history. After the war it served at various times as an opera house, an immigration station, and an aquarium. Today it attracts large numbers of visitors who tour the fort while waiting for a ferry to Liberty Island and the Statue of Liberty. Nowadays, Fort Wood is less well-known as an 1812-era fortification than as the platform on which Lady Liberty stands.

The British attack on Washington and Baltimore in 1814 not only struck at the heart of America but also helped unite the country. Ironically, the War of 1812 would be remembered not as a calamity that almost destroyed the nation but as a patriotic adventure. Americans still commemorate the war when they sing the National Anthem.

6

Chesapeake Theater
BATTLE FOR THE BAY

WHEN THE WAR OF 1812 BEGAN, President James Madison and other U.S. government officials understood that British warships might be able to reach Baltimore and other strategic Maryland and Virginia ports via the Chesapeake Bay. However, the bay made the politically and economically vital Chesapeake tidewater region far more vulnerable than they had ever imagined. Even Washington, D.C., the nation's capital, was open to attack from the sea, and as it turned out, could not be adequately defended by poorly trained militia.

By 1813, British warships had free run of the Chesapeake, where they blockaded ports, raided coastal communities, and expropriated supplies from tidewater farms. The Americans attempted unsuccessfully to fight back using militia and coastal gun emplacements, but U.S. naval resources were so limited that they had no reasonable hope of keeping the British out of the bay.

Into these trying circumstances strode a Revolutionary War hero by the name of Joshua Barney. He proposed a novel and relatively inexpensive means of defending Baltimore, Washington, and the Chesapeake as a whole. The U.S. would construct a fleet of shallow draft barges, which would be equipped with oars, sails, and a pair of powerful guns, one

The British, freed from their long struggle with Napoleon, sought to end their war with the United States with a series of powerful assaults. One of these was aimed at the Chesapeake Bay region, where the U.S. capital lay almost defenseless.

mounted in the bow and another in the stern. Barney believed that in the confined waters of the Chesapeake these small fighting craft could easily outmaneuver the big British warships. Barney envisioned his barges surrounding the enemy schooners and frigates like a swarm of angry hornets and driving them out of the bay.

Joshua Barney devised a unique plan for defending the Chesapeake with armed barges.

By April 1814, Barney had outfitted about two dozen of his barges at Baltimore, and he soon took them out into the Chesapeake to challenge the British. As it turned out, Barney's barges did not handle as well as he had hoped, especially in the open waters of the bay. They took on water and handled so awkwardly that Barney himself described them as "miserable tools." Even so, the British took Barney's little fleet seriously and prepared to meet it with a substantial force.

This chaotic illustration highlights key events during the British attack on Washington in the late summer of 1814.

On June 1, 1814, Barney's flotilla collided with Admiral George Cockburn's British fleet, which included the fourteen-gun schooner *St. Lawrence* (not to be confused with the ship of the line *St. Lawrence* launched at Kingston on Lake Ontario later that year) and a number of smaller vessels. More significantly, the British had nearby the HMS *Dragon,* a seventy-four-gun ship of the line likely capable of annihilating Barney's entire fleet with a single fire-belching broadside. The battle was over before it ever started. Seeing that he had no chance whatever, Barney ordered his boats to seek safety in the relatively shallow Patuxent River where he was sure the much larger British warships could not follow them.

As events would prove, the Patuxent was not as shallow as Barney had thought. Some of the British fleet managed to work its way into the river, driving Barney's barges further upstream. In doing so, the British became aware that the countryside roundabout the Patuxent was neither fortified nor defended with well-trained land forces. Thus began the sequence of events that would lead to what many still see as the war's climactic event.

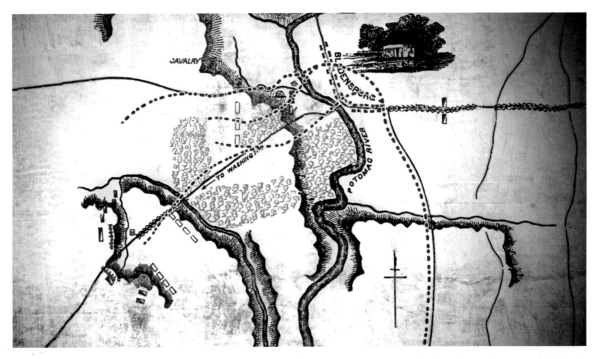

British troops approached Washington by marching north to Bladensburg where they swept aside a large force of American militia. The old map above traces the route of General Robert Ross's red-coated columns.

Once the war in Europe started to wind down in 1814, Britain planned to apply fresh military pressure to the United States aimed at forcing the Americans to capitulate. They hoped to end the war with a series of rapier-like thrusts. One of these would capture the important U.S. base at Plattsburgh, ending any possible threat to Canada. A second blow would fall upon the vulnerable Chesapeake region, where the British could strike their enemy's capitol and possibly burn Baltimore, one of America's most important centers of commerce.

In mid-August, Cockburn's flotilla, which had kept Barney bottled up in the Patuxent, was joined by a much larger fleet under Admiral Alexander Cochrane. Along with Cochrane came a large number of transports bearing approximately 5,000 experienced British regulars commanded by General Robert Ross. On August 19 the British troops disembarked at Benedict, Maryland, on the Putaxent and set out for Washington. Having burned their barges so that they would not be captured, Barney and his men hurried to Bladensburg, where they joined several thousand hastily assembled militiamen in an ill-fated attempt to block the British advance.

American defenses at Bladensburg were manned largely by lightly trained and badly equipped militia. Although the Americans outnumbered the British, they were poorly led and could not long stand in the face of well-directed assaults by Ross's red-coated regulars. Within three hours, American forces were in full retreat and the road lay open to the U.S. capital.

Later that same evening, just five days after they were put ashore, British soldiers strode unopposed down the broad avenues of Washington. There they burned the White House, the Capitol Building, and a number of other public and private structures. Then, late on the evening of August 25, the British marched out of the smoking city and eastward into the teeth of a howling storm.

Three weeks later the British launched yet another attack. This time their target was Baltimore, the third largest city in America after New York and Philadelphia, and the commercial heart of the entire tidewater region. Baltimore was also home to many of the privateers who had plagued British shipping throughout the war. By capturing and burning Baltimore soon after having driven Madison and his government from the nation's capitol, they hoped to end the war in circumstances highly favorable to the king's negotiators in Ghent.

Defended by ill-trained and poorly led militia, Washington was wide open to attack.

On September 12, Ross and his troops disembarked at North Point about a dozen miles southeast of Baltimore. Unbeknownst to the British, their forces had on the previous day suffered a major setback hundreds of miles to the north at Plattsburgh, New York, and they were about to be dealt another key reversal here in Maryland. By 8 a.m. Ross had formed up his forces and begun the march toward his objective. The British had not gone far, however, when they slammed into roughly 3,200 American militiamen under General John Stricker.

FRANCIS SCOTT KEY.

Francis Scott Key saw the successful defense of Baltimore's Fort McHenry as an intensely patriotic event.

Stricker's orders were to hold off the British as long as possible to provide more time for his comrades in Baltimore to organize the city's defenses. Indeed, Stricker and his outnumbered detachment managed to delay the British advance for several hours before finally being outflanked and forced off the field. The British then continued their march toward Baltimore, but without Ross who had been shot and killed in the fighting outside Northport. By the time the British regulars, now under the command of Colonel Arthur Brooke, reached the outskirts of the city, they found their path blocked by prepared defenses and nearly 10,000 militiamen.

Unable to dislodge such a large force, there was nothing for Brooke to do but hold his position and see if the Royal Navy could penetrate the city's harbor defenses. The key to those defenses was Fort McHenry, and the British placed it under rocket and cannon fire early on the morning of September 13. The firing went on throughout the day and all through the night.

Earlier, a Georgetown lawyer by the name of Francis Scott Key had gone aboard Admiral Cockburn's flagship to request the release of a friend who had been taken prisoner at Bladensburg. Of course, once the Battle of Baltimore was underway, neither Key nor his friend were allowed to leave, but were permitted to watch the unfolding drama from the deck of the ship.

It is likely that Key fully understood what was at stake. The Americans had been forced back at every turn on land. Their navy was bottled up in port and their economy had slowed to a standstill. New England was threatening secession. There could be little doubt about it— the United States was confronted by an utter and disastrous defeat, and if Fort McHenry fell and Baltimore with it, the disaster would be complete. The America that Key had known— and, perhaps, the one we know today as well—would surely be facing a less certain and more limited future. So it was that at dawn on September 14 Key looked anxiously toward Fort McHenry where on the previous evening he had seen an enormous battle flag fluttering in the breeze. Today, the people of three great nations, and much of the rest of the world besides, know well what he saw there in the early light.

Baltimore's Privateers

Among the reasons the British chose to attack Baltimore in 1814 was to punish that "nest of pirates" for having served as the homeport of numerous highly successful privateers. These privately financed armed vessels were licensed by the U.S. gov-

ernment to prey on British merchant ships. Captured ships and cargoes were sold for a profit, and privateer captains often grew wealthy on the proceeds. Royal Navy warships blasted or burned any privateers they caught at sea, but there was no shortage of seamen willing to run the risk. During the War of 1812, more than 500 U.S. vessels were licensed to act as privateers, and the British suffered enormous economic losses as a result. The value of lost British vessels and cargo has been estimated at more than $45 million. As many as 100 privateers operated from Baltimore alone. One of them, the 16-gun *Chasseur* under the command of Captain Thomas Boyle captured no fewer than fifty-three British prizes. It is said that Boyle amassed a fortune exceeding $1 million through his efforts as a privateer.

In 1814, swarms of sailors and marines from three British warships attempted to seize the American privateer General Armstrong, *which had dropped anchor in the Azores to take on water. Alert* Armstrong *crewmen managed to fight off the boarders but were later forced to scuttle their ship.*

HAVRE DE GRACE RAID
Havre de Grace, Maryland

FOLLOWING THE AMERICAN DECLARATION of war during the summer of 1812, the British did not immediately place the United States and its strategic Chesapeake Bay region under naval blockade. This was largely because they were still heavily engaged in their struggle with Napoleon and lacked the naval resources to cordon off the many navigable bays and estuaries along the U.S. coast. By the following year, however, the Royal Navy had begun to blockade American harbors and cut off the young nation's access to the sea. As part of this effort, a British fleet under the command of Admiral Cockburn sailed into the Chesapeake in early April of 1813.

At first, Cockburn attempted no large-scale raids, but his presence in the bay underscored the vulnerability of coastal communities in Maryland and Virginia. There seemed to be little the American army, navy, or militia could do to protect them. Toward the end of April, Cockburn made this painfully obvious by burning Frenchtown, which stood on the banks of the Elk River a few miles from the bay. The attack on Frenchtown enraged tidewater residents, who took to arms, determined to save their towns and villages from a similar fate.

While cruising in the far northern reaches of the Chesapeake near the mouth of the Susquehanna River, Cockburn's ships came under fire from an American shore battery on Concord Point. The cannonade proved largely ineffective but convinced Cockburn that he must silence these guns and punish the Americans for their defiance. On the night of May 1, Cockburn sent ashore approximately 150 marines who managed to take the town of Havre de Grace by surprise. The British burned much of the town, but their primary objective, the so-called "potato battery" on Concord Pont was not so easily overcome. This artillery emplacement had received its nickname because of the potato-size iron shot its small guns fired. The artillerymen on the point continued to blaze away at the British as long as they could. Even after all his comrades had fled, one especially stubborn local, a man named John O'Neil, still tried to serve his cannon. He was finally captured by Cockburn's marines. The British admiral threatened to hang O'Neil but later released him in recognition of his extraordinary fighting spirit.

WHAT YOU'LL SEE TODAY

A PAIR OF HISTORICAL MARKERS describing the attack on Havre de Grace can be found on Concord Point as well as an antique cannon said to have been used in the battle. O'Neil's quixotic one-man stand is also commemorated by an even more historic monument, the Concord Point Lighthouse. Built in 1827, the old stone tower and its still-active light are indirectly linked to the War of 1812 by O'Neil himself. As a reward for his considerable bravery, he was named keeper of the lighthouse, a post that remained in the O'Neil family for more than a century.

ST. MICHAELS RAID
St. Michaels, Maryland

DURING THE SUMMER OF 1814, Admiral Cockburn's fleet returned to the bay in force prepared to make life as unpleasant as possible for the Americans and hopefully compel them to surrender. The ultimate British objectives in the Chesapeake region were Washington, D.C., and Baltimore, its political and commercial nerve centers. However, even small ports such as St. Michaels on the Maryland eastern shore were not immune from harassment.

Early on the morning of August 10, 1813, a flotilla of British warships appeared off St. Michaels and opened up on the place with shot and shell. Unbeknownst to the Royal Navy gunners, they were aiming far too high to strike anything of consequence. Local home and business owners had hung lanterns in the tops of trees in hopes of convincing their attackers that these were the lights of buildings in St. Michaels. The deception worked, and only one structure was damaged. Two nights later, a second British assault was foiled, not by trickery but by determined fire from two local shore batteries.

WHAT YOU'LL SEE TODAY

HAVING SURVIVED A PAIR of British attacks, the town of St. Michaels itself is perhaps the most significant local monument to the War of 1812. The so-called Cannonball House on St. Mary's Square is said to have been hit by British artillery during the fighting. However, it is privately owned and is not open to the public. A few blocks away, the Chesapeake Bay Maritime Museum celebrates the history of St. Michaels and the entire tidewater region. St. Michaels can be reached by way of U.S. Highway 50 and Maryland Highway 33.

BLADENSBURG BATTLEFIELD
Bladensburg, Maryland

HAVING FORCED CAPTAIN JOSHUA BARNEY'S outgunned Chesapeake Bay Flotilla to retreat far up the Patuxent River, the British landed more than 4,000 regulars and marines at Benedict, Maryland. This substantial invasion force commanded by General Robert Ross then marched northwestward along a route that could be used as an approach to either Washington, D.C., or Baltimore. Ross hoped to confuse the Americans by keeping them in the dark for as long as possible regarding his ultimate objective. Having begun his advance on August 20, Ross reached the village of Bladensburg, a few miles north of Washington, on August 24. Ross and his men had pushed more than 40 miles into the heart of Maryland almost completely unopposed. In fact, over the course of a five-day march, they had barely seen an American soldier or militiaman.

Meanwhile, Barney and his men retreated overland toward Washington where they found U.S. government and military officials in a panic. The Americans had plenty of troops, perhaps as many as 10,000, with which to oppose the British. The problem was that they were scattered amongst small fortifications and farming communities all over the Maryland and Northern Virginia countryside. What was worse, the American forces were made up almost entirely of lightly trained militia. President Madison and his advisors knew, or should have known, that troops of this sort would stand no chance against British regulars, many of whom had previously taken the field against the armies of Napoleon Bonaparte in Europe.

Dolley Madison and White House servants saved Gilbert Stuart's portrait of George Washington from destruction by the British.

Dolley Madison

Dolley Payne Todd was a widow in her mid-twenties when she met and married Congressman James Madison. He was destined to become his nation's fourth president and to lead the country into one of its most trying conflicts. She was des-tined to become one of America's best loved and most famous first ladies. Unlike her far less gregarious husband in almost every way, Dolley Madison was an accomplished hostess, and her social talents did much to promote his political career. After he became chief executive in 1809, her invitations were coveted in Washington, where she continued to entertain and brighten spirits through the chaos of war. However, she is best remembered for her coolness in face of adversity and danger as the British closed in on Washington in August 1814.

When President Madison rode out to Bladensburg to access American defenses there, he left his official papers in his wife's safekeeping. She is credited with having saved from capture or destruction by British not only these important documents but also many nearly priceless White House valuables. Among the latter was the Gilbert Stuart portrait of George Washington, which had to be torn from its frame. With the papers, portrait, and many other valuable objects in tow, she entered a carriage and rushed off just ahead of the British. Later she was reunited with her husband at a roadside inn in Virginia.

By midday on August 24, some 6,000 American fighting men had gathered at Bladensburg. General William Winder, the U.S. commander, arrayed his forces in three long lines, stacked one behind the other. In front of the Americans ran the East Fork of the Potomac River.

The British approached the river from the southeast hoping to capture the Bladensburg Bridge intact. The Americans had prudently destroyed the other bridges that might have provided their enemies with more direct access to Washington. Shortly after noon, Ross ordered his men to rush the bridge, and after one failed attempt, they managed to establish themselves on the west bank. Soon thereafter, with the help of a firestorm of Congreve rockets, they outflanked the Americans and forced them back. Predictably, Winder's inexperienced militiamen could not stand up to the rockets and fixed bayonets of the British. Their retreat quickly deteriorated into a wild stampede that would later be described as the "Bladensburg Races." Retreating with the bulk of his soldiers was President Madison himself, who had ridden hard from Washington to witness this crucial encounter. He would ride even harder on his return trip.

The last Americans on the field were Barney and his sailors, whose artillery made the British pay a heavy price for their otherwise easy victory. In all, Ross's battalions lost nearly 250 killed or wounded compared to U.S. losses of about 50 men with 100 others captured. Unfortunately for the Americans, they had also lost the nation's seat of government. With Winder's army scattered to the winds, the door lay open to the capital, which the British entered later that same day. By the time the redcoats arrived, Madison and the other politicians who had helped start this war, and had thus far misdirected it, were long gone.

WHAT YOU'LL SEE TODAY

FOR REASONS THAT ARE LIKELY OBVIOUS, Americans have never gone to a great deal of trouble to commemorate the Battle of Bladensburg. There are no impressive monuments and no visitor's centers. A modest marker in Waterfront Park just south of the intersection of Annapolis Road and 46th Street tells the story of the battle while a plaque in Fort Lincoln Cemetery off the Bladensburg Road stands atop the hill where Barney and his men made their brave stand. Yet the battlefield is well worth a visit, if for no other purpose than to seek a reminder of the futility of war. The battle proved the ultimate humiliation for American arms, and Ross, the victor at Bladensburg, would be struck down by a sniper's bullet near Baltimore just three weeks later.

BURNING OF WASHINGTON
Washington, D.C.

ROSS'S MEN RESTED ONLY BRIEFLY before they began the seven-mile march to Washington, which they reached on the evening of August 24. Before the night was over, fire had consumed the White House, the as-yet-unfinished Capitol Building, and a large number of other public and private structures. Many of the fires were intentionally set by the British in retaliation for the burning of York by American troops the previous summer. Others were started by accident or by retreating American troops attempting to keep gunpowder and other valuable stores out of British hands. The British nonetheless captured large quantities of military supplies and equipment.

It would seem that Ross's assault on Washington had been an unqualified success. President Madison and other government leaders had been driven into the countryside, and the nation's capitol city had been put to the torch. However, the British had not gained the one, most precious objective they might have hoped to achieve—a decisive and favorable end to the conflict. In many, if not most wars, events such as those that took place at Bladensburg and Washington on August 24-25, 1814 would have forced the surrender of a vanquished nation, but not in this case. The British likely understood that the Americans, who only a generation earlier had endured far worse calamities along the road to winning their independence, would probably keep fighting. Ross and Admiral Cockburn knew they would have to drive home their advantage if they hoped to win the peace through force of arms. Their next stop would be Baltimore, a city of far more commercial and strategic importance than Washington.

WHAT YOU'LL SEE TODAY

IT IS A WIDELY SHARED OPINION that every American child should visit Washington, D.C., at least once. There is scant room here to list the nearly countless valuable lessons, historical and otherwise, the city and its monuments have to teach. Certainly, there is no better place to put into perspective that bizarre and yet somehow wondrous chapter of American history that unfolded between 1812 and 1815. The fact that the city exists at all as the capital of the United States is in some ways a monument to the War of 1812.

This pastoral image of Washington, D.C., suggests that the U.S. capital city was actually little more than a country town at the time of the British attack.

The White House, famously located at 1600 Pennsylvania Avenue, was handsomely restored after the war and remains to this day the home of American presidents. Under its sparkling white coat of paint, however, remain the coal-black scars of vengeance extracted by the British two centuries ago. Tours of the White House, usually available only through a congressman, offer an opportunity to consider the American experiment in nationhood, which though still developing, has been by and large successful. While walking through the publicly accessible rooms, it is also possible to imagine Ross's redcoats outside with their torches and Dolley Madison desperately scurrying about trying to save whatever she could from the enemy.

The Capitol Building, which occupies what would be the intersections of Pennsylvania and Maryland Avenues, was also blackened during the burning of Washington. Lacking its well-known rotunda, the 1814 structure looked very little like it does today. The sandstone and marble building, which had been under construction since 1793, did not burn readily, and a providential rainstorm saved it from complete destruction. The House and Senate meeting chambers were restored and ready for use by 1819, and the remainder of the structure, including the rotunda was completed seven years later. Although extensive design changes and reconstruction have altered the building's appearance over the years, it stands amongst the most recognizable structures in the world. Displays on the first floor include relics from the War of 1812 and the British assault of Washington.

These paintings show the U.S. Capitol Building before and after the British put it to the torch.

Not burned during the brief British occupation of the city was the U.S. Marine Barracks at 8th and I Streets. Consequently, several of the original military post buildings still stand, and they are among Washington's oldest existing structures. Although the historic complex remains part of an active military facility, it is open for tours on Wednesdays.

A few blocks west along the grassy National Mall from the Capitol Building is the National Museum of American History. Perhaps foremost among its displays is the most famous artifact leftover from the War of 1812—or perhaps any war—the enormous battle flag that flew above Fort McHenry during the Battle of Baltimore. It is, of course, known to nearly everyone as the Star-Spangled Banner.

NORTH POINT BATTLEFIELD
Dundalk, Maryland

FROM THE BRITISH POINT OF VIEW, the capture and destruction of the U.S. capital at Washington, D.C., had only been a sideshow. The vibrant city of Baltimore had always been their ultimate strategic objective in the Chesapeake Theater. About three weeks after their victory at Bladensburg, the British, under the overall command of Admiral Cochrane, launched the assault they hoped would bring a swift end to the war. Their fleet gave them an enormous advantage in mobility, and they had used it with devastating effect on the Patuxent. Now they would use it again to surprise and outflank the American defenders at Baltimore.

The British plan for their Baltimore campaign was a relatively simple one. General Ross would put his men ashore at North Point and then march upon the city from the east rather than from the south as the Americans might have expected. It was hoped that the British fleet could provide support by sailing along the north shore of the Patapsco River, but as it turned out the shallow waters made this impossible. However, Ross believed that if he could catch the Americans by surprise, he might not need any help from the big Royal Navy guns. So, early on the morning of September 12, Ross and his 4,000-man invasion force set out from North Point and marched toward Baltimore about fourteen miles away.

British Admiral George Cockburn mercilessly burned and looted small towns along the Chesapeake before accompanying General Robert Ross during his destructive raid on Washington and ill-fated march on Baltimore.

About halfway to their objective the British came up against an American defensive position that had been hurriedly established by General John Stricker and 3,200 Maryland militiamen. The American lines lay across a narrow neck of land between the waters of the Back River to the north and Bear Creek to the south, completely blocking the road to Baltimore. When General Ross rode forward to see if he could find a way to outflank Stricker, a shot fired by an American sniper struck him in the chest. Ross died soon thereafter, having handed over command to Colonel Arthur Brooke.

Brooke understood that time was against him. He had to reach Baltimore before the defenses there were made so strong that he would have no hope of overcoming them. Consequently, he ordered an immediate assault. Supported by artillery fire and screaming Congreve rockets, the British moved forward. The majority of Brooke's troops were regulars, some of

A British warship bombards a Chesapeake coastal community.

whom had fought under Wellington at Waterloo. The militia facing them were mostly farmers, laborers, and shopkeepers, few of whom had much in the way of formal military training. Nonetheless, they managed to hold off the British long enough to prevent them from reaching Baltimore that day.

By 4 p.m. Brooke's redcoats had driven back Stricker's militia with both sides having suffered heavy casualties. The British then pitched camp for the night. When they attempted to resume their advance the following morning, it soon became obvious that the defenses around Baltimore were now too well prepared to be taken by storm. The outcome of the campaign now depended on the results of the artillery duel by that time in progress between Admiral Cochrane's ships and the steadfast gunners at Fort McHenry.

Shallow water and the determined fire of American gunners forced the British to bombard Fort McHenry from a considerable distance. The fortress was the key to Baltimore's defenses, and the long-range salvos of shot and shell failed to subdue it.

WHAT YOU'LL SEE TODAY

TODAY, MARYLAND HIGHWAY 151 and the Patapsco Parkway pass right through the North Point Battlefield where two centuries ago the fate of so many hung in the balance. A plaque located near the village of North Point off Old North Point Road commemorates the battle. Nearby is a monument marking the spot where General Ross is said to have fallen. Interestingly enough, the monument is not dedicated to Ross but rather to Aquilla Randall, a young American sharpshooter believed by some to have fired the bullet that killed the British commander. Ross's military accomplishments are celebrated by an impressive obelisk-style memorial in his native Northern Ireland, but it should come as no surprise that, even today, the general receives little positive mention in Maryland. In 1814, a Baltimore newspaper described Ross as "the leader of a host of barbarians," his killing as "the just dispensation of the Almighty," and his men as "a new race of Goths, outraging the ordinances of God and the laws of humanity."

FORT MCHENRY
Baltimore, Maryland

BUILT IN THE SHAPE OF A FIVE-POINTED star around the turn of the nineteenth century, Fort McHenry was named for James McHenry, a signer of the U.S. Constitution and Secretary of War under President John Adams. The fort's heavy guns made it extremely difficult, if not impossible, for Admiral Cochrane's fleet to approach Baltimore's Inner Harbor where they could provide telling support for a ground assault on the city. With Brooke's troops stalled miles short of their objective, Cochrane knew he would have to capture Fort McHenry or abandon the Baltimore campaign.

Beginning at first light on the morning of September 13, the British fleet opened up on the fort from near maximum range. Over the next twenty-five hours, the British pounded the fort's thick brick walls with nearly continuous barrages of solid shot, mortar shells, and Congreve rockets. Fired from as much as 3 miles away, most of the 1,500 or so rounds sent hurtling shoreward missed their mark, and those that struck home did little serious damage. Nor could the twenty-four-pound and thirty-two-pound cannonballs lobbed at the British from Fort McHenry find their marks. Even so, the firing went on in earnest throughout the night. It must have been a truly impressive fireworks display. When it ended around 7 a.m. on September 14, Cochrane signaled his ships to retire down the river toward the Chesapeake. Brooke ordered his troops to march back to North Point, where they re-boarded their transports. The Battle of Baltimore was over.

WHAT YOU'LL SEE TODAY

FORT MCHENRY IS PERHAPS America's best known and loved historic structure dating from the War of 1812. The fort reminds visitors of American resilience at what may have been the nation's darkest hour. Now part of the Fort McHenry National Monument and Historic Shrine, the pentagon walls, barracks, and other period structures have been extremely well restored. Fort McHenry can be reached from downtown Baltimore via the Francis Scott Key Highway and East Fort Avenue.

Almost as old as Fort McHenry and even more popular with tourists is the USS *Constellation*, permanently docked in Baltimore's attractive Inner Harbor area. Although she saw very limited action during the War of 1812, this often restored frigate on display in Baltimore's Inner Harbor is nonetheless a must-see for visitors. Children and, more often than not, their parents as well, are awed by this two-century-old windjammer. Like the USS *Constitution* in Boston, the *Constellation* offers visitors an up-close look at navy life during the early nineteenth century.

Also in the Baltimore area are the Rodgers Bastion Plaque marking the fortified defensive line that helped hold back the British; the Star-Spangled Banner Memorial; the Flag House, home of Mary Pickersgill, the seamstress who made the thirty-two-foot by forty-two-foot flag that flew over Fort McHenry; the Francis Scott Key Monument; the Battle of Baltimore Monument downtown; and several other sites commemorating the city's defense.

North Wind Picture Archives

Official U.S. Army uniforms like these were scarce at the Battles of Bladensburg and North Point, where most of the American forces consisted of militia. These lightly trained citizen soldiers performed poorly at Bladensburg but put up a good fight outside Baltimore.

One of the bloodiest battles of the war took place outside New Orleans on January 8, 1815, two weeks after peace negotiators had agreed to terms at Ghent, Belgium. British General Edward Pakenham is shown above leading an all-out attack on American positions while General Andrew Jackson lifts his sword to encourage the defenders. Neither man realized the war was officially over, and Pakenham died in the attack. Jackson survived and was later elected President of the United States.

7
Southern Theater
CANNON BEFORE NEW ORLEANS

MUCH OF THE FIGHTING DURING THE War of 1812 took place in the north along the border between the United States and Britain's Canadian provinces, on the open ocean, or in the Chesapeake Bay. Even so, leaders on both sides understood that the key to overall victory might very well be found not in the North but in the South. Thus, especially toward the end of the war, the attentions of the combatants turned southward. Ironically, the outcome of the fight for the South would not be known for certain until the war—though not the killing and dying—had supposedly ended.

President Madison and Secretary of State James Monroe were both Southerners. When they led the nation into open conflict with Great Britain during the summer of 1812, they were no doubt aware that the South would be at risk in any protracted struggle. New Orleans, the indispensible key to the Mississippi and the as-yet-unexploited Louisiana Territory, would be especially vulnerable. With an optimism that to this day gives pause to serious students of history, Madison, Monroe, and the War Hawks who had pressed them to act largely ignored such considerations. They assumed that Canada would be in American hands and the war long over before the British and their Indian allies proved a serious threat to either the South or other regions of the country. They were wrong.

Departing Jamaica in late November 1814, the British landed a substantial force in the bayou country to the east of New Orleans.

Once it began to appear that the war would not be over quickly, the Madison Administration took its first halting steps toward a strategy for protecting Louisiana and the South as a whole. To shore up coastal defenses and help protect New Orleans, General James Wilkinson was placed in command of U.S. forces along the Gulf of Mexico. Consisting of a few scattered units totaling fewer than 1,700 men and a handful of small gunboats, the American military in the South was weak. By no stretch of the imagination could it have withstood a determined invasion by the British. Alarmed by this state of affairs, Wilkinson called for substantial reinforcements, as many as 10,000 additional troops and 40 gunboats.

What Wilkinson received instead of the reinforcements he sought was an order to occupy Spanish Florida. This was a mission he could not possibly achieve with the meager resources at his disposal. Even so, in April 1813, Wilkinson managed to take the strategic port of Mobile with just a few hundred troops and a small flotilla of gunboats. Soon thereafter, he was promoted to major general and reassigned to the Canadian border region, where his spotty performance would eventually get him kicked out of the army.

As it turned out, the British threat to the South was not as great as it may have appeared, at least not during the early years of the war. The fighting against Napoleon in Europe and the defense of Canada left the British without the ships and troops necessary for any worthwhile ventures elsewhere. However, the threat of Indian attack was very real indeed. Tecumseh's potent appeals had won over many Native American converts, especially among the Creeks who lived in small towns and villages along southern rivers. As many as 4,000 Red Stick Creeks rose in rebellion, launching bloody attacks on isolated forts and farming settlements. The rebels were called "Red Sticks" because of the red war clubs carried by creek warriors and also, perhaps, because of the supposedly magical red sticks said to have been carried by some Creek shamans.

To deal with the rebellion, several Southern states called out their militias. The most effective of these forces was the Tennessee militia commanded by General Andrew Jackson,

Andrew Jackson, shown here in his general's uniform, took firm charge of the New Orleans defenses.

who marched into the Creek heartland with about 2,500 men, among them the young Sam Houston and Davy Crockett. Having defeated Red Stick war parties in a number of sharp encounters, Jackson managed to destroy much of the Creek food supply. Then, on March 27, 1814, Jackson's campaign against the Indians reached a climax at Horseshoe Bend on the Tallapoosa River, where he thoroughly defeated and broke the power of the Red Sticks.

Three months after Horseshoe Bend, Jackson was appointed commander of all U.S. military forces in the southern theater. Establishing his headquarters in Mobile, Jackson then sought to strengthen his hold on the Gulf coast by extending U.S. conquests in northwestern Florida. In November his troops took the Spanish outpost of Pensacola, about 50 miles east of Mobile.

Interestingly enough, Jackson had been ordered by administration officials not to attack Pensacola and thus run the risk of bringing Spain into the war on the side of Great Britain. However, the letter containing the order did not reach the general's hands for months, in fact, not until the war was over—an indication of how remote the Gulf region was from decision makers in Washington and London.

Meanwhile, Admiral Cochrane had concocted a rather elaborate southern strategy to win the war for Britain. He would attack and temporarily occupy the small state of Rhode Island. Then, while the Americans were scrambling to respond, he would hurry his warships and troop transports to the Gulf of Mexico and attack New Orleans. With this key to the entire continental interior in his pocket, Cochrane was sure he could quickly force the United States to surrender.

Perhaps because the attacks on Washington and Baltimore were considered sufficient diversions, the Rhode Island part of Cochrane's plan was abandoned. But late in 1814, the campaign in the South proceeded in earnest. In early December a large British fleet appeared off the coast of what is today the state of Mississippi. A few days later, British forces under Cochrane and General John Keane forced their way into Lake Borgne east of New Orleans and then marched on the city itself. On December 23, Keane and a British vanguard of about 1,800 troops reached the east bank of the Mississippi River. There they pitched camp and settled down to await reinforcements, but they would get no rest that night.

Aware that the British might be planning an attack, Jackson had rushed westward from Mobile to take charge of the defenses around New Orleans. There he was soon joined by a force of 2,500 armed militiamen who had hurried down the Mississippi from Tennessee. When he received word that the enemy was camped a day's march from the city, Jackson acted quickly. Accompanied by as many men as he could muster, he hit them with a surprise night assault. Supported by the guns of a small American schooner anchored in the river, the attack stunned the British and threatened to drive them into the marshes. However, the arrival of a fresh regiment helped Keane avert disaster, and before morning he had regained control of his camp. Both sides had lost more than 200 killed, wounded, or missing in a nightmarish struggle in which it was seldom possible to tell friend from foe.

Jackson's troops retreated about 3 miles northward to the Chalmette Plantation. Although Keane continued to receive reinforcements from Lake Borgne, he was apparently unaware that his army now greatly outnumbered the Americans. So, instead of immediately pushing forward to New Orleans, he held his position. This decision would prove fateful—and fatal to thousands of his men—since it allowed Jackson to consolidate and strengthen his lines at Chalmette.

On Christmas Day, loud cheers could be heard rising from the British camp by the river. The ovation was not in celebration of the holiday but rather to greet the arrival of a large body of reinforcements. With these fresh troops came Sir Edward Pakenham, who had been sent by British military officials to take charge of the Louisiana invasion. General Pakenham immediately took over command from the badly shaken and uncertain Keane and began to assess the situation.

Andrew Jackson on his charger

An English aristocrat and brother-in-law to the Duke of Wellington of Waterloo fame, Pakenham was a capable tactician. He had at his disposal nearly 14,000 men, more than three times the number now available to Jackson. This substantial force should have been more than sufficient to overwhelm the defenses of New Orleans, except that Pakenham could not get there. To reach the city, he had to puncture Jackson's lines at Chalmette Plantation.

At Chalmette, Jackson had scraped together a largely untrained force of approximately 4,000 men. They were as unlikely a body of troops as ever took the field under the command of a U.S. officer. Amongst them were frontiersmen from Tennessee and Kentucky, freed black slaves and creoles, French- and Spanish-speaking planters and fishermen, Choctaw warriors, and perhaps even pirates who had served under the swashbuckling Captain Jean Laffite. Jackson placed his riflemen behind well-prepared earthworks and established eight separate batteries of heavy field artillery to support them. The American defensive works would prove all but impenetrable when Pakenham finally put them to the test.

After weeks of trying—and failing—to find a way around Jackson's strongly defended position, Pakenham launched an all-out frontal assault. On the morning of January 8, 1815, several thousand brightly clad British soldiers fixed bayonets and stepped off in strict parade-ground formation toward what the Americans called Line Jackson. Marching across at least a quarter mile of open ground, the British were cut down in droves by American cannon and rifle fire. Among those who fell was Sir Pakenham himself, who was blasted off his horse by grapeshot from an American cannon. With Pakenham dead, the battle soon ended. It had cost the British almost 2,000 killed, wounded, or captured. Jackson had lost fewer than 100 men.

The American army that defeated the British at New Orleans was extraordinarily diverse. It included, for instance, Tennessee and Kentucky frontiersmen, local planters, Indians, and freed black slaves.

Andrew Jackson's Revenge

There may be no more colorful a character in American History than Andrew Jackson. Born in 1767 to Scots-Irish parents who had immigrated to the Carolinas a few  years earlier, he was caught up in the American Revolution as a young teenager. Captured by the British, he was beaten and struck in the head with a sword for refusing to clean an officer's muddy boots. The experience left him with a permanent scar across his forehead—and in his soul. Although he nearly died from smallpox while imprisoned by the British, he survived and vowed that someday he would take vengeance on them. Jackson's opportunity for revenge would come many years later in Louisiana.

Anti-British feelings still burned brightly in Jackson's breast when he arrived in New Orleans late in 1814. The general's iron will and passionate spirit electrified the city as he hurriedly established an intelligence system and went around patching up defenses. With his hated enemies, the British, approaching from the south, Jackson recruited to his army everyone who was willing to fight and some, perhaps, who were not so willing.

"Those who are not for us," said Jackson, "are against us, and will be dealt with accordingly."

The troops that rallied to Jackson's banner proved so diverse that he had his orders translated into French, Spanish, and Choctaw. Even though they might not always have understood one another, Jackson's troops responded to his stirring call: "Fellow citizens of every description! Remember for what you contend. For all that can render life desirable, for a country blessed with every gift of nature, for property, for life, and for liberty, dearer than all..."

Jackson's rough frontier eloquence would serve him well when the critical moment—and the neatly arrayed red ranks of British soldiery—came at Chalmette Plantation on January 8, 1815. His men stood firm and delivered to the British Army one of its worst single-day defeats in history. That same eloquence would later serve Jackson in politics as well and carry him, more than fifteen years after the Battle of New Orleans, to the presidency.

The British remained in Louisiana for a few more weeks, then boarded their ships and departed. The Battle of New Orleans was over and so, finally, was the War of 1812. Unknown at the time to anyone in Louisiana, the terms of peace had been agreed upon at Ghent more than two weeks earlier. In fact, the negotiations were successfully concluded on Christmas Eve, the day before Pakenham arrived with his reinforcements on the banks of the Mississippi. However, peace treaties do not often neatly conclude major conflicts, and certainly this was the case with the Treaty of Ghent and the War of 1812.

It has been said that, having taken place after the war had officially ended, the Battle of New Orleans was essentially meaningless. Nothing could be further from the truth. Had the British succeeded in taking New Orleans, they could have used it to promote the rise of a Native American nation in the Midwest, the establishment of which had been one of their chief war aims. They might even have held onto New Orleans, despite the treaty terms, and in this way frustrated the ambitions of a troublesome United States. Indeed, Pakenham had arrived carrying a British commission naming him the new governor of Louisiana and authorizing him to establish a new British-Spanish civil government in the region. But, of course, none of this came to pass.

Because Jackson and his remarkably diverse army turned back the British, the door of the West remained not just ajar but wide open to U.S. expansion. Indeed, the War of 1812, of which the Battle of New Orleans was the final episode, made possible the United States we know today. It also made possible the Canada we know today, and in a very real sense, the Britain we know today as well.

Having won the last battle, Americans were able to tell themselves that they had won the war itself—despite the burning of Washington and the many defeats along the Canadian border and elsewhere. Having repulsed every American invasion attempt, Canadians believed and, with good enough reason, continue to believe to this day that *they* won the war. And though their defeat in Louisiana might sting, the British never for a moment believed that *they* had lost. Instead, they emerged from the war the mightiest and most prosperous nation on earth, and that is hardly the fate of a defeated people.

For all these reasons, the War of 1812 did not sow the seeds of future wars, and that is cause for celebration. In fact, there is much to celebrate in what the War of 1812 was—an assertion of national pride and identity—and in what it never became—a war of conquest and annihilation. It is likewise well worth celebrating what we, the peoples of three great nations, have learned during the two centuries since the war ended at Ghent and at Chalmette Plantation. We have found that there is far greater profit in standing together as brothers than in facing one another as foes.

Vanished Native American Dream

The American, British, and Canadians all came out of the war believing they had won or, at the very least, had not lost. However, there was one group of combatants that clearly did lose: America's native peoples, particularly those in the Midwest. Tecumseh's dream of a Midwestern confederacy of native tribes died with him on the Thames. Along with it died the last real hope that Native Americans might somehow resist the tide of white settlers inundating their lands and their culture. As the British left Fort Mackinac—in accordance with the terms of the Treaty of Ghent—their Indian allies watched in shock. Chief Sausamauee of the Winnebago cried out: "Father! You promised us repeatedly that this place would not be given up. It would be better that you had killed [us] at once, rather than expose us to a lingering death."

NATCHEZ TRACE

Tupelo, Mississippi

BEFORE THE NINETEENTH CENTURY, the American Midwest was almost entirely devoid of roads. People and goods moved from one place to another by water, and fortunately, a vast network of rivers and streams were available to make transportation possible. Even so, the lack of roads delayed development of the continental interior and made settlement of the region more difficult for Easterners and Europeans. Of course, the Mideast and the Mississippi Valley would not remain a trackless frontier forever.

By the nineteenth century, white traders and settlers had begun to use an old Indian forest trail that linked the Cumberland and Mississippi Rivers. Shortly after he took office in 1801, President Thomas Jefferson ordered the U.S. Army to enlarge and improve the trail to encourage western commerce and settlement. Within a few years, the Natchez Trace, which stretched 444 miles from Nashville to Natchez, had become a heavily traveled thoroughfare.

Much of the American West was a trackless wilderness with few roads of any kind. Little more than a crude trail, the Natchez Trace linking the Cumberland and Mississippi Rivers was used by Andrew Jackson to move troops toward New Orleans.

Early in 1813, Andrew Jackson led a small army of Tennessee "volunteers" down the trace to Natchez. Their objective was Louisiana, where Jackson believed they were needed to defend New Orleans from imminent attack by the British. Apparently, Jackson also had it in mind to seize Florida from the Spanish. Convinced that no British attack was coming and that it would be a grave mistake to antagonize Spain, U.S. military officials ordered Jackson to return with his men to Nashville.

WHAT YOU'LL SEE TODAY

NOWADAYS A FEDERALLY OWNED and maintained parkway follows the approximate route of Natchez Trace. The tree-lined roadway stretches the entire distance from Nashville to Natchez, and driving it at the posted speed limit of fifty miles per hour can take the better part of two days. There are no fuel stations or restaurants and very few buildings of any kind along the Trace, but services can be found a short distance beyond most of the exits. A National Park Service visitor center complete with museum is located in Tupelo, and historic sites can be seen at various locations along the Trace.

FORT CONDE
Mobile, Alabama

BUILT IN 1723 TO PROTECT THE important coastal settlement of Mobile, Fort Conde was at various times held by the French, British, Spanish, and American militaries. Built of brick, stone, earth, and cedar, the fort was an impressive structure covering almost 11 acres. It was the site of a significant Revolutionary War battle in 1780 when Spanish troops and their American allies forced the British garrison to surrender.

Fort Conde was possessed by Spain until April 15, 1813, when General Wilkinson seized Mobile. Moving five gunboats in close to the fort, Wilkinson surrounded it with his militia and demanded the surrender of its small garrison. Severely outnumbered and outgunned, the Spanish commander felt he had no choice but to comply. Andrew Jackson would later use the fort as a base during his campaigns at Pensacola and New Orleans.

WHAT YOU'LL SEE TODAY

FORT CONDE WAS COMPLETELY demolished in 1823 to make room for the fast-growing port city of Mobile. The fort was largely forgotten until the 1970s when archeologists excavated the site and then restored a portion of its walls. The fort seen today was constructed on a slightly smaller scale than the original. Located near the corner of Royal and Church Streets near the Mobile waterfront, the fort houses the city's official welcome center.

HORSESHOE BEND
Tallapoosa County, Alabama

IN MARCH 1814, GENERAL JACKSON and his Tennessee militia struck the blow that would soon bring an end to the Creek rebellion in the South. Having previously used hit-and-run tactics against the whites, the rebel Red Stick Creeks had finally decided to make

A Creek Chief

a stand against Jackson's advancing army. They took up a strong defensive position at a horseshoe-shaped peninsula formed by a sharp bend of the Tallapoosa River in what is now eastern Alabama. Led by a fierce war chief named Manawa, about 1,000 Red Sticks dug entrenchments across the open end of the horseshoe and there awaited Jackson.

When the Tennesseans arrived on March 27, Jackson immediately recognized that, instead of preparing an ambush for his men, the Indians had constructed a death trap for themselves. After pounding the mostly exposed Red Sticks with artillery for more than an hour, the militia charged the Indian earthworks. The Indian defensive line soon gave way, but the Red Sticks had nowhere to retreat. More than 800 of Manawa's warriors were slaughtered in the desperate hand-to-hand fighting. Jackson lost only 26 of his militiamen.

Their power utterly broken, the last of the Red Sticks held out for several months in the wilds before surrendering to Jackson in August. The treaty signed by the Creeks at Fort Jackson near present-day Montgomery, Alabama, ceded millions of acres of land to the U.S. government. The fame he won at Horseshoe Bend and later at New Orleans would eventually propel Jackson to the presidency. Two decades later as President, Jackson would deal harshly—some would say treacherously—with the Cherokee Indians who had fought alongside his militia against the Red Sticks.

The Creek people occupied a wide swath of the Deep South.

WHAT YOU'LL SEE TODAY

THE 2,040 ACRE HORSESHOW BEND National Military Park near Dadeville, Alabama, encompasses the site of this crucial frontier battle. A visitor center and museum located off Alabama Highway 49 helps put the battle in perspective. Historical markers at various points on the battlefield describe the fighting.

BATTLE OF NEW ORLEANS
New Orleans, Louisiana

BRITAIN'S INVASION OF LOUISIANA was the final sharp, stabbing point of a three-pronged pincers attack intended to drive the United States out of the war. The first two prongs thrust up the Chesapeake Bay to Washington and Baltimore and down Lake Champlain to Plattsburgh. As we have seen, these two efforts produced mixed results, and to an extent, were intended as diversions. The most important element of the overall British campaign was in essence a flanking attack aimed directly at New Orleans. In part by chance and in part because of General Jackson's keen tactical sense, the focus of the

177

According to a widely accepted legend, Jackson's troops at Chalmette Plantation fought from behind bales of cotton. Actually, their well-prepared defenses consisted mainly of dried mud and timber parapets. Cleared fields beyond the American works left the advancing British in the open, where they were cut down like stalks of corn.

British push on the strategic Mississippi River port became a narrow neck of mostly dry ground about 9 miles south of the city.

Although the British could have marched on New Orleans as early as December 23, 1814, they delayed the attack for more than two weeks to allow slow-moving reinforcements to reach the area. This gave Jackson time to gather reinforcements of his own and to strengthen his defenses at Chalmette Plantation. Jackson's lines at Chalmette Plantation stretched about a mile from the Mississippi on his right to an impassable cypress swamp east of the river. The American fortifications consisted of a mud parapet some five feet high punctuated by a series of heavy gun emplacements. In front of the parapet was a moat-like ditch and beyond that a broad expanse of flat fields that had been cleared of trees, shrubs, and plantation buildings. Once the battle started, this open ground would become a killing field.

Warships and gunboats add the roar of their cannon to the din of battle at New Orleans. British naval superiority failed to provide them with an edge, and their defeat on the banks of the Mississippi brought the War of 1812 to a resounding and definitive close.

The Battle of New Orleans began in deadly earnest just after dawn on January 8, 1815. As the British marched in their orderly ranks toward Jackson's parapet, they were cut down like so many stalks of cane. In the finest tradition of the British military, General Pakenham rode among his troops encouraging them to press onward until he was scythed from the saddle by American cannon fire. Command of the attacking British forces then fell to General John Lambert, who, seeing his men being needlessly slaughtered, ordered them to retreat. The battle had lasted about two hours and resulted in a lopsided victory for the Americans.

Having lost heart along with thousands of their best troops, the British soon withdrew from the banks of the Mississippi and from Louisiana. Although fought after the war was officially over, the battle had profound consequences for all concerned. It discouraged any further challenges on the part of the British to U.S. sovereignty over the Midwest, the Mississippi basin, and the Louisiana Territory. Perhaps more importantly, it enabled the

Word of peace is never so fondly received as by ordinary people. This painting depicts a rowdy assemblage of Americans getting the good news.

American public and Republican political leaders to claim with some small justification that the United States had won the war or, at the very least, had not lost it.

WHAT YOU'LL SEE TODAY

THE CHALMETTE BATTLEFIELD AND CEMETERY enable visitors to relive this important—some might say pivotal—battle, if only in their imaginations. Some of the battlefield has been swallowed up by the wandering Mississippi, but what remains is evocative of the past and eerily beautiful. The ruins of the American earthworks and of the canal that served Jackson's troops as a moat can still be seen. Markers describe the action and interpret key points of interest. A striking feature of the battlefield is the Chalmette Monument, which was begun in 1840 and not completed until 1908. The marble monument rises over 100 feet above the surrounding river floodplain. The battlefield is located a few miles south of New Orleans on Louisiana Route 39.

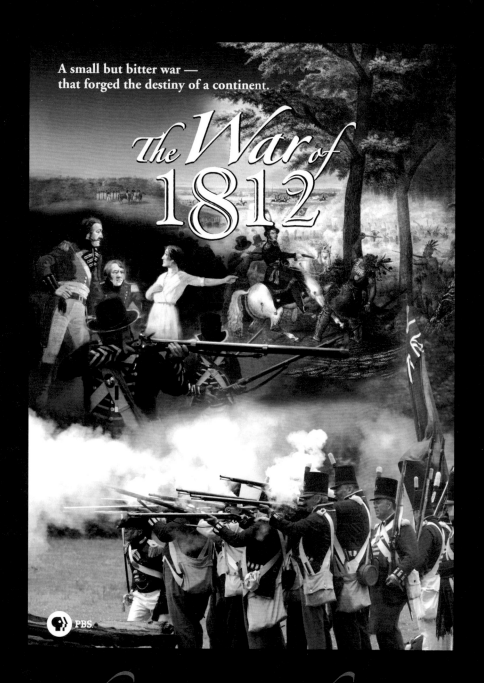

A small but bitter war —
that forged the destiny of a continent.

The War of 1812

PBS

The War of 1812

A GUIDE TO BATTLEFIELDS AND HISTORIC SITES
is the official companion book to the exciting PBS documentary
The War of 1812. For more information on historic destinations
related to the War of 1812, visit www.pbs.org/1812.

Bibliography

Akins, Thomas. *History of Halifax City*. Halifax: Nova Scotia Historical Society, 1895.

Andrews, Roger. *Old Fort Mackinac on the Hill of History*. Menominee, WI: Leander Press, 1938.

Babcock, Louis. *The War of 1812 on the Niagara Frontier*. Buffalo, NY: Buffalo Historical Society, 1927.

Ballard, William. "Castine, October 1, 1814." *Bangor Historical Magazine*, 1996.

Barbuto, Richard. *Niagara, 1814: America Invades Canada*. Lawrence: University of Kansas Press, 2000.

Beirne, Francis. *The War of 1812*. New York: E.P. Dutton, 1949.

Black, Jeremy. *The War of 1812 in the Age of Napoleon*. Norman: University of Oklahoma Press, 2009.

Borneman, Walter. *1812: The War that Forged a Nation*. New York: Harper Collins, 2007.

Bowler, Arthur. *War along the Niagara*. Youngstown, NY: Old Fort Niagara Association, 1991.

Brant, Irving. *James Madison*. Indianapolis: Bobbs-Merrill, 1961.

Brooks, Charles. *The Siege of New Orleans*. Seattle: University of Washington Press, 1961.

Brown, Roger. *The Republic in Peril*. New York: Columbia University Press, 1964.

Carter, Samuel. *Blaze of Glory: The Fight for New Orleans 1814-1815*. London: Macmillan, 1971.

Clark, Thomas. *A History of Kentucky*. Lexington: University of Kentucky Press, 1960.

Cleaves, Freeman. *Old Tippecanoe*. New York: Charles Scribner and Sons, 1939.

Collins, Gilbert. *Guidebook to the Historic Sites of the War of 1812*. Toronto: Dundurn, 2006.

Compton, Smith. *The Battle of Queenston Heights*. Toronto: McGraw-Hill, 1968.

Dillon, Richard. *We Have Met the Enemy: Oliver Hazard Perry*. New York: McGraw-Hill, 1978.

Dunnigan, Brian. *The British Army at Mackinac, 1812-1815*. Lansing, MI: Mackinac Island State Park Commission, 1980.

Engleman, Fred. *The Peace of Christmas Eve*. New York: Harcourt, 1962.

Ewing, Frank. *America's Forgotten Statesman: Albert Gallatin*. New York: Vantage Press, 1959.

Forester, Cecil Scott. *The Age of Fighting Sail: The Story of the War of 1812*. Sandwich, MA: Chapman Billies, 1956.

Fredriksen, John. *Officers of the War of 1812*. Lewiston, NY: Edwin Mellan Press, 1989.

Gardiner, Robert. *The Line of Battle*. Annapolis, MD: Naval Institute Press, 1992.

Gilpin, Alec. *The War of 1812 in the Old Northwest.* East Lansing: Michigan State University Press, 1970.

Harvey, D.C. "The Halifax-Castine Expedition." *Dalhousie Review* 18, 1938-1939.

Heidler, David Stephen. *Encyclopedia of the War of 1812.* Santa Barbara, CA: ABC-CLIO, 1997.

Hickey, Donald. *The War of 1812: A Forgotten Conflict.* Chicago: University of Illinois, 1989.

Horsman, Reginald. *The Causes of the War of 1812.* Philadelphia: University of Pennsylvania Press, 1962.

Ingraham, George. "The Story of Laura Secord Revisited." *Ontario History* 57, 1965.

Jenkins, Wheeler. "The Shots that Saved Baltimore." *Maryland Historical Magazine* 77, 1982.

Kirby, William. *The Annals of Niagara.* New York: Macmillan, 1927.

Knopf, Richard. *The War of 1812 in the Northwest.* Columbus: Ohio State Museum, 1960.

Lord, Walter. *The Dawn's Early Light.* New York: W.W. Norton, 1972.

Mahon, John. *The War of 1812.* Gainesville: University of Florida Press, 1972.

Malcomson, Robert. *A Very Brilliant Affair: The Battle of Queenston Heights.* Annapolis, MD: Naval Institute Press, 2003.

Marrin, Albert. *1812: The War Nobody Won.* New York: Atheneum, 1985.

Millett, Alan, and Peter Maslowski. *For the Common Defense.* New York: The Free Press, 1984.

Molotsky, Irvin. *The Flag, the Poet, and the Song: The Story of the Star-Spangled Banner.* New York: Dutton, 2001.

Morton, Desmond. *A Military History of Canada.* Toronto: McClelland and Stewart, 1985.

Mullaly, Franklin. "The Battle of Baltimore." *Maryland Historical Magazine* 54, 1959.

Perkins, Bradford. *The Causes of the War of 1812.* New York: Rinehart and Winston, 1962.

Pratt, Julius. *Expansionists of 1812.* New York: Macmillan, 1925.

Randdall, Thomas. *Halifax: Warden of the North.* Toronto: McClelland and Stewart, 1974.

Remini, Robert. Henry Clay: Statesman for the Union. New York: W.W. Norton, 1992.

Roosevelt, Theodore. *The Naval War of 1812.* New York: Putman's Sons, 1900.

Sanford, John. "The Battle of North Point." *Maryland Historical Magazine* 24, 1929.

Shomette, Donald. *Flotilla: The Patuxent Naval Campaign in the War of 1812.* Baltimore: Johns Hopkins University Press, 2009.

Skeen, Carl Edward. *Citizen Soldier in the War of 1812.* Lexington: University of Kentucky Press, 1999.

Stanley, George. *Battle in the Dark: Stoney Creek.* Toronto: Balmuir Book Publishing, 1991.

Sugden, John. *Tecumseh's Last Stand.* Norman: University of Oklahoma Press, 1985.

Suthern, Victor. "The Battle of Chateauguay." *Canadian Historic Sites* 11, 1974.

Tucker, Spencer, and Frank Reuter. *Injured Honor: The Chesapeake-Leopard Affair.* Annapolis, MD: Naval Institute Press, 1996.

Whitefield, Carol. "The Battle for Queenston Heights." *Canadian Historic Sites* 11, 1974

Index

Photographs and Illustrations

The War of 1812 was fought two centuries ago when no photography was available to record key events or preserve images of the politicians, generals, soldiers, sailors, or civilians caught up in the conflict. For that reason this book relies on art and modern photography to visually bring the war to life for readers. This could not have been accomplished without the invaluable assistance of numerous re-enactors, photographers Meike Zuiderweg, Stephen McCarthy, and Catherine Thompson, and public or private archives in the United States and Canada. Most of the archival artwork was made available by the Library of Congress, the Library and Archives of Canada, the National Portrait Gallery, the Government of Ontario Art Collection, and other libraries, museums, or agencies. Several of the colorful historic prints that appear throughout the book were supplied by North Wind Picture Archives. Photo and illustration credits are as follows:

Copyright page (top and bottom): Meike Zuiderweg; page iv: Meike Zuiderweg; page viii: Amit Sethi; page 1: Corcoran Gallery of Art; page 3: Library of Congress; page 4: Library and Archives of Canada; page 6: Amit Sethi; page 8 (left): Toronto Reference Library; page 8 (right): National Portrait Gallery; page 9: Indiana Historical Society; page 10: Library of Congress; page 12 (left): White House Historical Association; page 12 (center): Library of Congress; page 12 (right): National Portrait Gallery; page 14: Library of Congress; page 16: Meike Zuiderweg; page 18: Library of Congress; page 20: Smithsonian American Art Museum; page 22: Library of Congress; page 23: Library of Congress; page 24: Library of Congress; page 26: Library and Archives of Canada; page 27: Library and Archives of Canada; page 28: Library of Congress; page 30: Florentine Films/Hott Productions; page 32: Library of Congress; page 35: Amit Sethi; page 37: U.S. Senate Commission on Art; page 39: Library of Congress; page 41: Government of Ontario Art Collection; page 42: Amit Sethi; page 43: National Portrait Gallery; page 45: University of Michigan Clements Library; page 47: Florentine Films/Hott Productions; page 48: Florentine Films/Hott Productions; page 49: Library of Congress; page 50: Stephen McCarthy; page 52: United States Naval Academy Museum; page 53: Library of Congress; page 54: Toronto Reference Library; page 55: Western Reserve Historical Society; page 57: Library of Congress; page 59: Library and Archives of Canada; page 60: Government of Ontario Art Collection; page 62: Archives of Ontario Library; page 63: Library and Archives of Canada; page 64: Library of Congress; page 65: Government of Ontario Art Collection; page 66: Library and Archives of Canada; page 68: National Gallery of Art; page 71: Wikimedia Commons/Balcer; page 72: Meike Zuiderweg; page 74 (left): Library and Archives of Canada; page 74 (right): Library and Archives of Canada; page 76: Old Fort Niagara; page 78: Meike Zuiderweg; page 79: Brown University Library; page 81: Library of Congress; page 82: Government of Ontario Art Collection; page 84 (top and bottom): Meike Zuiderweg; page 89: New York Public Library Phelps Stokes Collection; page 90: Library of Congress; page 92: Florentine Films/Hott Productions; page 95: North Wind Picture Archives; page 97 (top): United States Army Art Collection; page 97 (bottom): Library of Congress; page 98: Fort York; page 99: Fort York; page 101: Library of Congress; page 102: Library of Congress; page 103: Library of Congress; page 104: Meike Zuiderweg; page 105: Library of Congress; page: 106 Catherine Thompson, The Chesterville Record; page 108: Meike Zuiderweg; page 109: Library of Congress; page 110: Florentine Films/Hott Productions; page 112: Chateau Ramezay Museum; page 113 (top): Historic Columbia Foundation; page 113 (bottom): Chateau Ramezay Museum; page 114: National Portrait Gallery; page 115: Catherine Thompson, The Chesterville Record; page 118: Meike Zuiderweg; page 120 (top): Chateau Ramezay Museum; page 120 (bottom): Florentine Films/Hott Productions; page 121: Amit Sethi; page 122: Library of Congress; page 124: Library of Congress; page 126: Florentine Films/Hott Productions; page 128: Florentine Films/Hott Productions; page 129 (left and right): Library of Congress; page 130: Library of Congress; page 131: Library of Congress; page 132: Monroe County Historical Commission Archives; page 135: North Wind Picture Archives; page 137: Library of Congress; page 139 (top and bottom): Library of Congress; page 142: Library of Congress; page 144 (top): Amit Sethi; page 144 (bottom): Library of Congress; page 145: Library of Congress; page 146: Amit Sethi; page 147: Library of Congress; page 148: Library of Congress; page 149: Pride of Baltimore, Inc. (pride2.com); page 150: Library of Congress; page 153: Library of Congress; page 154: Library of Congress; page 157: Library of Congress; page 158: Library of Congress; page 159: Library of Congress; page 160: North Wind Picture Archives; page 161: Library of Congress; page 163: North Wind Picture Archives; page 164: Library of Congress; page 166: Amit Sethi; page 167: Library of Congress; page 169: Library of Congress; page 170: Historic New Orleans Collection; page 171: Library of Congress; page 173: Library of Congress; page 174: Florentine Films/Hott Productions; page 176: Library of Congress; page 177: Library of Congress; page 178: Historic New Orleans Collection; page 179: Library of Congress; page 180: Toledo Museum of Art.